COOKING

with His

LOVE

A JOURNEY OF FAITH & HOPE WHILE EXPERIENCING THE NAMES OF GOD

Chef Julio 12/1/14.

Chef JULIO RUBIO

I DEDICATE THIS BOOK TO THE FOLLOWING:

To my Master Chef, Jesus Christ! I have come to know that, without Him, I am truly nothing. Thank you for choosing me and allowing me to be a part of Your kingdom. "You did not choose Me, but I chose you and appointed you that you should go and bear fruit, and that your fruit should remain, that whatever you ask the Father in My name He will give you. ~Jesus Christ (John 15:16)

To my brother, Marlon Rubio, who was there to help me pick up the pieces and was so instrumental in leading me to my faith in Jesus Christ. I am so blessed to have you not only as my brother but also a faithful friend.

To Pastor Glenn Harvison, Pastor Nick Uva, and my Harvest Time Church family for your love and encouragement. I would not be where I am today without the words of life that you have spoken over me, the prayers you have prayed for me, and the many ways you have supported me while at Harvest Time and beyond.

ACKNOWLEDGEMENTS

A very special thank you to my wife, *Emily Rubio*, for your support and devotion to me from the start. I know that God has put us together so that we can be a powerhouse couple for His kingdom. I am blessed to have you at my side. I love you with all my heart!

Thank you, *Christina Viafore*, photographer, for your commitment and willingness to be a part of my book project.

Thank you, *Max Murphy, Pat Reynolds and Suzanne Weaver*, for your help in reviewing the book. Your support and encouragement enable me to keep going and never to give up. You are my true friends.

Thank you, *Sue Palmer*, editor, for sharpening the text of my manuscript with such excellence. You were truly a Godsend! My wife and I have surely been blessed with a gem of a friend, whose relationship with us will only continue to grow.

TABLE OF CONTENTS

FOREWORD

I first met my friend, Julio Rubio, several years ago when he began coming to services and events at our church in Connecticut. He was one of the most earnest people I had ever met–a wonderful mixture of a man who was both highly focused on doing God's will and yet lighthearted no matter his circumstances. I'm not sure the English language has a word for this type of person, so I'll just say that Julio is joyfully serious.

Julio is serious about his relationship with God, and it shows in his everyday life. A talented chef, many times I've heard him refer to God as his "Master Chef." I'd never heard the Almighty referred to in this fashion before, but now that I know Julio it makes perfect sense to me. Whether in or out of the kitchen, Julio views his work and his relationships as offerings, creations to be offered to a very special judge who will know if he prepared them with enough love. Of course, he's also serious about food itself, diligently and creatively working on recipes as any good chef does. We're so happy for the recognition his labors have earned him of late and we know his star will continue to rise.

Julio is also joyful. He knows the joy of having triumphed through tears, and having overcome losses. He knows the wonder of seeing the world through new eyes, and seeing what was burned to the ground begins to spring back into what the Bible calls "newness of life." In gratitude to the God who rescued him, Julio combines his love of cooking with a desire to see other people receive new hope, the same hope that propelled him on a journey to recover wholeness in his own life.

This book is about that journey. Very skillfully, the author shows us how he experienced the grace of God in a new way on every leg of his road back. Julio learned that the Bible ascribes many different titles to God–each Divine Name conveying its own particular insight into His goodness. Along his unique path to recovery, Julio was beholding these different facets of the Lord's love, and discovering that God could be trusted to keep leading him into a good future. Tracing Julio's voyage from rock bottom all the way back to where he'd been and beyond, you will see that God really is a Master Chef. He took the unlikely ingredients of a man's life and made from them a miraculous, new creation. God was the first one to "cook with love," and it's made all the difference in Julio's life.

Listen to Julio Rubio as he explains how God's love can make the same difference for you. This book is for anyone who needs hope. You may be in the grip of a serious addiction. Perhaps you've lost family, friends, or a career because of a bottle of pills or a bottle of liquor. You've seen others throw it all away and yet you're not sure you have the power to end up any different. Maybe you've never known the love of a caring father and you're empty on the inside. Whatever kind of loss might have touched your soul, Julio's story will inspire you to see that there is a living God who knows you by name and is able to make something beautiful out of your life.

Read, eat, enjoy!

Rev. Nick Uva
Harvest Time Church
Greenwich, Connecticut

INTRODUCTION

To call someone by name is a sign that you know that person on some level. Some of my friends know me as "Julio." Others call me by my middle name, "Cesar." If I hear both names being called, I turn my head instantly. That's because they're using the name only very close friends and family use.

I think our Heavenly Father does the same thing when we call him by one of His special names. If we have a need and cry out "Jehovah Jireh," for example, He bends His ear a bit closer because the one crying for provision clearly knows Him. Similarly, if you are in need of healing and cry out "Jehovah Rapha," He responds to you, knowing you realize He is the One who heals. Whatever your specific need may be, our Heavenly Father has a name tied to His character that can respond to that need.

Not only do the names of God speak of His nature; they also tell us something about how he desires to relate to His people. How awesome is that! It is my hope that, through this book, you'll not only find tasty recipes that cause you to thankful to the Creator of the feast, but you'll be inspired to know and see His character reflected in the lives of those who love Him.

Following each chapter, in which you will see God evidencing Himself by one of His names, you will find a menu dedicated to that name. It is my hope you will use that menu to draw together a group of your friends together for a special dinner and time of meditation or discussion about the names of God. What great way to bring honor to His name!

Most ingredients in each recipe are organic because our Heavenly Father's nature is truly organic. He only displays who He is in the truest form. His love and ways are given to us in their purest forms. Ask the Holy Spirit to give you a side dish to go along with each main dish that will inspire your guest or your family. Read the story of that specific name and have your guest tell the story of how that name of God has been seen in your life.

No doubt about it, *Cooking with His Love* will bring the very nature of God in your home as you begin to meditate and call out His specific name. Let the Heavenly Father inspire you to use this book in making His name famous.

As my friend Pastor Nick says, *"Read, Eat and Enjoy!"*

Chapter One

ELOHIM
God My Creator

Genesis 1:27
"So Elohim created humans in his image. In the image of
Elohim he created them. He created them male and female."

*H*aving a beer was considered cool growing up in "the 'hood" in Yonkers, NY, so, not surprisingly, I was introduced to alcohol when I was still a young teenager. Unfortunately, I didn't know how addictive alcohol could be or how much destruction it could cause.

Soon, alcohol became such a part of my life that, when my consumption of it became an addiction, I didn't even notice it. I was, however, slowly going out of control.

Before I knew it, alcohol had so consumed me that I could no longer function at work. I had no job. My family, too, could no longer tolerate being around me. They shut the door on me.

With nowhere to go, and no human being to sustain me, I found myself on the streets. A successful chef who once delighted in serving his patrons tasty entrees had now been reduced to begging for money on the streets to feed his addiction. I was sleeping on park benches and under bridges, along with stray cats and dogs. Nothing was appealing. I was just surviving.

One spring night, I began to plot my demise. I decided the quickest and most painless way was to jump off the Tappan Zee Bridge. As I was walking toward the bridge, I replayed the suicide over in my mind. Just then, I heard an unfamiliar voice, a still small voice, speaking to me in a very authoritative, yet pleading manner. "Go and get help."

I didn't know at the time whose voice I had heard, and, quite frankly, I didn't care. I just knew I wanted, even needed, to follow. But where should I go? A second thought came to mind: "Go to the medical hospital." So, with a bottle of liquor hidden inside my jacket, I went.

After arriving at the hospital, I sat in the emergency room waiting area for about 45 minutes, struggling with my thoughts. Amazingly, even though I was at the end of my rope, I was still contemplating whether this were the right decision. Getting help would also mean letting go of the alcohol I was using to cope with life. What would I do without it? Fortunately, before I had the chance to give into my fears and run, the nurse saw me and reached out to me.

Little did I know that this was the beginning of my road to freedom with my Creator, Elohim, the One whose voice I'd miraculously heard in my time of need, the God who created me and formed me in my mother's womb (Psalm 139), who gave me life and had a plan for me. Elohim (which means "Strong One" in Hebrew) had rescued me and I would never be the same again!

Isaiah 44: 24
"Yahweh has reclaimed you. He formed you in the womb. This is what Yahweh says: I, Yahweh made everything. I stretch out the heavens by myself. I spread out the earth all alone."

ELOHIM MENU

Soup:
Tomato Soup

Salad:
Greek Salad

Fish Entree:
Mexican Red Snapper

Meat Entree:
Arroz Con Pollo

Vegetarian Dish:
Mushroom Ceviche

Dessert:
Flan

Prayer:

Thank you Father, my Elohim, who has created everything for me.
Thank you for this meal and all the ingredients that comes from
your creation. God you have blessed me with every blessing
and we thank you for all that you have created.
Amen

Tomato Soup
(Serves 8)

4 cups of organic Vegetable juice
4 cups of organic Tomato juice
1 whole organic Spanish onion cut into small-diced pieces
2 Tablespoons of organic raw Coconut oil
4 clove of organic Garlic, minced
2 cups of organic Carrots cut into small-diced pieces
1 cups of organic Celery small-diced
2 organic Bay Leaves
1 cup of organic Soymilk
5 Whole organic Basil leaves
1 Tablespoon of organic Spanish Smoked Paprika
1 teaspoon of organic kosher Sea Salt
1 teaspoon of organic Black Pepper
1 Tablespoon of organic Raw Honey

1. Use a 5-quart saucepan heat oil over high heat and add the onions, carrots, celery and garlic. Cook until softened for approximately 3 minutes.
2. Add the tomato juice, vegetable juice and bay leaves and bring it to a boil.
3. Add the milk and bring it to a simmer. Then add the basil leaves and whisk it together and discard bay leaves.
4. Add the remaining ingredients and with a hand blender to puree the soup. Cook for about 15 minutes and serve.

Greek Salad
(Serves 8)

8 cups of organic chopped Romaine
1 large organic seedless Cucumber, slice in half moon
5 large organic Tomatoes medium diced
1 cup of organic Tomatoes medium diced
1 cup of organic Red Onions small diced

5 cups of organic canned Red Lentil rinsed & drained
7 Tablespoons of organic real Lemon juice
3 teaspoons organic extra Virgin Olive Oil
1 Tablespoons kosher organic Black Pepper
1 cup of organic chopped fresh Oregano
2 teaspoons of organic Red Sea Salt
3 teaspoons of organic fresh chopped Mint

1. In a large salad bowl toss, all the ingredients accept the lemon juice olive oil and seasoning.
2. Take 8 salad bowls and equally arrange romaine salad into the salad bowls then drizzle the lemon juice, oil and seasoning topped with feta cheese is optional and serve.

Mexican Red Snapper
(Serves 8)

8 (6 oz.) Red Snapper fillets, boneless
2 Tablespoons of fresh organic Lime Juice
1 cup of organic kosher Non-alcoholic White Wine
2 teaspoons of organic Sea Salt
2 teaspoon of organic Black Pepper
4 Tablespoons of organic raw Coconut Oil
2 cups of organic Spanish onions, thinly slice
2 Tablespoons of organic Minced Garlic
6 cups of organic fresh Tomatoes, small diced
2 cups of organic Fish Broth
1 cup of organic slice Black Olives
4 Tablespoons of organic Cilantro, chopped
2 teaspoons of organic fresh Mexican Oregano
2 organic Bay Leaves
2 Tablespoons of organic Jupiter Capers thinly slice
4 large organic Serrano Peppers, Seeds removed and slice thinly

1. Marinated the snapper in the non-alcoholic wine, lime juice and salt for 30 minutes.

2. Heat oil in a large skillet over medium heat then add onion until cook golden brown.
3. Add the remaining ingredients bring to a simmer for about 20 minute or until the sauce is semi-thick.
4. Add the fish to the sauce, cover until the snapper is cooked and serve.

Arroz con Pollo
(Serves 8)

2 cups of organic White Rice Raw
4 cups of organic Chicken Broth
1 pound of organic free rage Chicken Cutlet, medium chunks
1 cup of organic Green Peas
1 cup of organic Spanish Onions, small diced
2 teaspoons of organic Mexican Ground Cumin
2 Tablespoons of organic Olive Oil
2 teaspoons of organic Ground Coriander
2 Tablespoons of organic fresh Cilantro, chopped finely
1 teaspoons of fresh Saffron

1. In a large medium saucepot add the olive oil; bring it to a medium heat. Add the chicken chunks sautéed for about 5 minutes, or until they are golden brown.
2. Then add all the ingredients and cook for about 30 minutes and serve.

Mushroom Ceviche
(Serves 8)

6 cups of organic fresh Lobster Mushroom quartered
1 cup of organic Red Onions chopped finely
2 Tablespoons of organic minced Garlic
1 teaspoon of organic kosher Sea Salt
1 teaspoon of organic White Pepper

2 organic Serrano Peppers finely chopped
1 Tablespoon of organic Mexican fresh oregano roughly chopped
1 Tablespoon of organic Cilantro roughly chopped
1 cup of organic fresh squeeze Lime Juice
2 Tablespoons of organic Olive Oil
½ cup of organic Red Bell pepper, small diced
½ cup of organic Green Pepper, small diced
1 cup of organic chopped Black Olive

1. In a large mixing bowl put all the ingredients and refrigerate for about 3 hour.
2. Chill 8 Martini glasses put equal amount of the chill ceviche topped with lemon wedges for garnish and serve.

Flan

Flan
(Serves 8)

8 Tablespoons of organic Sugar
8 organic Brown Eggs
2 teaspoons of organic Vanilla Extract
2 strips of organic Lemon Peels
2 organic Cinnamon Stick
4 cups of organic soy Almond Milk
1 teaspoon of Sea Salt
8 teaspoons Caramelized Sugar
1. Bring milk to a boil with lemon peel and cinnamon.
2. Lightly beat eggs with a wire whisk and blend in the sugar, vanilla extract, and salt.
3. Take caramelized sugar and pour 1 teaspoon on the bottom of each custard cup.
4. Add milk gradually, strain and pour into ovenproof custard cups in a pan of hot water (2 inch deep) and bake in oven for 55 minutes at 300 degree.
5. Remove from pan and cool the custard cups in refrigerator to serve. Remove from custard cups by taking a butter knife and cut around the edges then turning upside down. Spoon caramelized sugar from bottoms of the cups over top of each custard.

Caramelized Sugar

1. 2 cups of organic sugar
2. 2 Tablespoon of fresh bottled water
3. Heat and melt together

JEHOVAH RAPHA
God My Healer

Chapter Two

JEHOVAH RAPHA
God My Healer

Exodus 15:26
"He said, "If you will listen carefully to Yahweh your Elohim and do what he considers right, if you pay attention to his commands and obey all his laws, I will never make you suffer any of the diseases I made the Egyptians suffer, because I am Jehovah Rapha."

"How can I help you?" the nurse asked.

"I am drunk and I have suicidal thoughts," I replied.

The nurse stated, "We have to get you in now!"

They took me to a room for observation because I was intoxicated. I was wearing filthy clothes and the hospital staff replaced them with a clean hospital gown. I had a brand new bottle of rum hidden inside my jacket. I was trying to secure my bottle, as I wanted to make sure I got my money's worth. However, the hospital attendant heard the bottle when I dropped my jacket to the floor. " What do we have in here?" he asked as he took the bottle from the pocket inside my coat. Shortly after, security came to retrieve the bottle of liquor. My filthy clothes that reeked of an unbearable odor were stripped from me and my bottle of liquor was gone. Now truly I had nothing left. I felt numb.

Minutes seemed like hours and the alcohol began to wear off. I began to feel angry and upset because it seemed like forever being in that room. I asked the nurse, "What is taking so long?" She replied that I needed to be in the room because I was intoxicated and they needed to wait for a room in the psychiatric ward.

After a few hours, I was admitted and began to go through the process of detoxification, which would last for a few days, none of them pleasant. Vomiting, the shakes, loss of appetite, and emotions of fear, loneliness, and hopelessness surfaced. It was horrible!

There were other issues besides physical ones to contend with, as well. Fear settled in: the fear of knowing what I had become and the fear of the unknown plagued me. I was at rock bottom. Yes, I was getting help now, but what would happen after that? My family didn't want me. I had no place to go. It was really scary.

Despite my fears, I pressed on. I stayed at the hospital, submitting to the care of the psych ward staff, attentively following their instructions and advice. A social worker was also assigned to me, whose job was, among other things, to review my progress.

Six weeks later, I started to see some real, positive changes in my life. I was becoming a different person. Life was becoming more meaningful. I began to be aware of my surroundings and took notice of those who were helping me. Submitting to those whose hands I was presently in taught me to structure my day and learn how to live normally again.

I knew my time at the hospital was coming to and end.

When the hospital staff finally told me I was free to go, I panicked. "I don't want to go out there!" I told the social worker. "If I do, I'll return to alcohol, the very thing that brought me here!"

The social worker looked at me, then asked: "Are you telling me that you're looking for further help?" "YES!" I shouted.

More help would be difficult to find, the social worker admitted, since I had no identification and no insurance.

He assured me, however, that he would do his very best to assist me.

In my heart, something told me that help would come from somewhere, somehow. I told him that I would stay here in the hospital until he found something for me.

About a week later, the social worker came to see me. There was a bed in a rehabilitation facility in upstate New York, he told me. It was a long-term facility, he explained. Once I was admitted, I would be in there for a long time. Was this really what I wanted, he wondered? Without hesitation, I again said, "Yes." Within three days I was being transported in a white van to upstate New York.

Some healings are instantaneous and some are a process. Mine was definitely of the latter kind. It was so gradual, in fact that I didn't even realize that my healing process had begun. But it had. It began the day I chose to obey that "still small voice" (I Kings 19:12) and "go get help" as my Jehovah Rapha (which means "The Lord my Healer" in Hebrew) had told me. In doing so, I had begun my journey to a place of healing and freedom from my addiction. Thank you, Jehovah Rapha, for all the healing You have given and continue to give me. Apart from You, I can do nothing!

Psalms 103:2-5
"Praise Yahweh, my soul, and never forget all the good he had done: He is the one who forgives all your sins, the one who heals all your diseases, the one who rescues your life from the pit, the one who crowns you with mercy and compassion, the one who fills your life with blessings so that you become young again like an eagle."

JEHOVAH RAPHA
MENU

Soup:
Chicken Soup

Salad:
Caesar Salad

Fish Entree:
Stuffed Flounder with Crabmeat

Meat Entree:
Veal Scaloppini Marsala

Vegetarian Dish:
Broccoli Mac & Cheese

Dessert:
Berries Fritters

Prayer:

I praise you Jehovah Rapha that you are my God who heals. As we break bread, will you blessed this food to our bodies. We pray that you will heal all sickness and diseases with each person here. Thank you for the price you paid for our healing.
Amen

Chicken Soup
(Serves 8)

4 pounds of organic Chicken parts
8 cups of organic Chicken broth
1 cup of organic Celery cut into medium dice pieces
1 cup of organic Spanish onion cut into medium dice pieces
1 cup of organic Carrots cut into medium dice pieces
½ cup of organic Parsnip cut into medium dice pieces
2 organic Bay Leaves
2 Tablespoons of organic Italian curly parsley
1 Tablespoon of organic Cilantro finely chopped
1 teaspoon of organic Garlic powder
1 teaspoon of organic Black Pepper

1. Place the chicken parts and the chicken broth in a 5quart soup pot. Bring it to a boil skimming off the fat that rises to the top. Lower the heat let it simmer for 30 minutes or until the chicken is done.
2. Remove the chicken from the pot, put it aside so that will cool off then, add the rest of the ingredients to the pot let it simmer for 30 minutes. Go back to the chicken remove the meat from the bone and add it to the soup and serve.

Caesar Salad
(Serves 8)

8 cups of Organic Romaine Lettuce
16 ounces of Organic Plain Croutons

1. Chopped Romaine medium bite size clean and dry thoroughly. Hold refrigerated until ready to serve.
2. Set croutons and hold until ready to serve.

Caesar Salad

Dressing

1 teaspoon of organic Garlic paste
4 organic Anchovy Fillets
1 teaspoon organic kosher Sea Salt
1 teaspoon organic Black Pepper
2 ounces organic whole Eggs
2 ounces organic fresh squeeze Lemon Juice
10 ounces organic virgin Olive Oil
8 ounces organic grated Parmesan cheese

1. Add garlic, Anchovy's seasoning and eggs, lemon juice and blend. Add olive oil whisking to form a thick dressing.
2. Portion the chopped Romaine on 8 cold plates topped it with Caesar dressing Parmesan cheese and croutons and serve.

Stuffed Flounder with Crabmeat
(Serves 8)

8 (6 ounces) Flounder Fillets
1 teaspoon of organic Black Pepper
1 teaspoon of organic kosher Sea Salt
2 cups of organic all-purpose Flour
2 cups of organic Liquid Eggs
3 cups of organic Japanese Panko Bread Crumbs
2 cups of organic Coconut Oil
1 cup of melted organic Butter
½ cup of fresh organic squeeze Lemon Juice

1. Trim the flounder.
2. Fill each fillet with a portion of crabmeat stuffing and roll the fish around the stuffing. Overlap the edges to form a seam.
3. Roll the flounder in the flour, dip in liquid egg and roll in breadcrumbs.
4. Heat ½ amount of butter or oil at about medium heat. Add the flounder to the hot oil. Pan fry for about 2 minutes on each side, or until internal temperature reaches 145°F. Topped with melted butter and lemon juice and serve.

Crabmeat stuffing
(Serves 8)

20 ounces of Crabmeat or organic Crabmeat
1 Tablespoon of organic minced Shallots
4 ounces of organic medium chopped Green onions
2 ounces of organic unsalted Butter
3 ounces of organic all-purpose Flour
8 ounces of kosher organic Non-alcoholic White Wine
8 ounces of organic Soymilk
2 teaspoons of organic chopped Parsley
1 teaspoon of organic kosher Sea Salt
1 teaspoon organic Black Pepper

1. Pick through the crabmeat removing any bits of shells or cartilage.
2. Fold in all the ingredients and form 8 medium size balls and stuffed the flounder fillets.

Veal Scaloppini Marsala
(Serves 8)

4 pounds of boneless 6 oz portion free rage veal top round
1 teaspoon of organic kosher Sea Salt
1 teaspoon organic Black Pepper
organic Flour as needed
organic Coconut Oil as needed
1 cup of Non-Alcoholic White Wine for deglazing as needed
3 cups of Marsala Sauce

1. Cut veal top round and portion it out into 8 portions. Pound it with a meat mallet between plastic wrap to a thickness of ¼ inch think. Season it and flour the cutlets lightly immediately before sautéing.
2. Heat the pan and add the oil and sauté the veal for a about a minute and half per side until medium or desired doneness. Remove the veal from the pan keep warm.
3. Plate the veal topped it with 2 oz of Marsala Sauce and served.

Marsala Wine Sauce

1 ounce organic Shallots finely minced
2 sprigs of organic Thyme
1 organic Bay Leaf
1 teaspoon of organic Black Peppercorns
1 cup of organic kosher Non-Alcoholic Red Wine
3 cups of organic DEMIGLACE (find it in your whole foods store near you)

1 cup of organic kosher Non-alcoholic Marsala Wine
1 teaspoon of organic kosher Sea Salt
1 teaspoon of organic Black Pepper

1. Combine the shallots, thyme, bay leaf, peppercorn, and non-alcoholic red wine. Reduce by half over medium heat.
2. Add the DEMIGLACE and continue to simmer until the sauce has developed a good consistency.
3. Add the non- alcoholic Marsala wine and simmer. Season the sauce strain the sauce into a clean pan.

Broccoli Mac-Cheese
(Serves 8)

1 pound of organic Elbow Macaroni
5 ounces of the organic Butter
2 organic Spanish onions, finely chopped
6 Tablespoons of organic plain Flour
4 cups of organic Coconut Milk
4 teaspoons of organic Brown Mustard
16 ounces of fresh organic Broccoli Florets
4 ounces of organic Japanese Panko Breadcrumbs

1. Cook pasta in boiling salt water for 7 minutes and drain. Preheat the oven to moderate 350°F and grease casserole dish.
2. Melt the butter in a large saucepan over heat and cook the onions for 10 minutes, or until softened. Stir in the flour and cook for 2 minutes until pale and brown. Remove from the heat and gradually stir in the milk.
3. Return to the heat and stir until the sauce boils and thickens. Reduce the heat and simmer for 3 minutes, stir in the mustard, add about ½ amount of the cheese and season to taste.
4. Mix the pasta with the cheese sauce. Transfer into a casserole dish and sprinkle the breadcrumbs and the remaining cheese over the top. Bake for 20 minutes or until golden brown and bubbling.

Berries fritters
(Serves 8)

2 organic eggs
1 ounce of organic Sugar
6 fl ounces of kosher Non-Alcoholic White Wine
6 fl ounces of organic Pear Juice
1 teaspoon of organic kosher Sea Salt
½ teaspoon of organic Lemon Zest
12 ounces of organic all-purpose Flour
2 pounds of organic fresh Blueberries
2 pounds of organic Black Berries
Coconut oil for frying
20 fl ounces organic Fruit Sauce
6 fl ounces of organic Whipped Cream

1. Combine the eggs and sugar in a mixing bowl, with a hand blender beat lightly at medium speed.
2. Add the wine, pear juice, salt and lemon and grapefruit zest and combine all together.
3. Add the flour and blend until smooth.
4. Dip the berries in the batter and deep fry at 350°F until golden brown. Place on paper towels.
5. Serve with fruit sauce and whipped cream.

JEHOVAH EL ROI
My God Who Watches Over Me

Chapter Three

JEHOVAH EL ROI
My God Who Watches Over Me

2 Chronicles 16:9
"Yahweh's eyes scan the whole world to find those whose hearts are committed to him and to strengthen them."

It took two-and-a-half hours to drive from the hospital to the rehab facility. As we were riding along, I remember fear was creeping in. The thought of whether or not I was making the right decision was running repeatedly through my mind. I was not the only person in the van entering rehab that day. Others were in the van, probably having the same thoughts and similar fears. We were all asking each other for a cigarette, but no one had one.

Upon entering the facility, we were stripped and searched to ensure that there was no hidden contraband. They checked everywhere and everything. I had very few belongings with me so the process was not long. I had no clothes and still was wearing the scrubs that were given to me from the hospital. The only personal belonging I had was a little bag from the hospital, which consisted of toiletries, socks and underwear.

The rehab staff took me to a room that had Goodwill clothing. I looked to see what would fit me and ended up with brightly colored, mismatched outfits that should not even *be* together, but I didn't care. It was so good to have clean clothes, other than hospital garments, on my body.

They showed me to my room, which I shared with six other guys. Since I was the "newbie" on the block, I was given the top bunk. Soon it was clear to me that to be popular in the group, you had to have contraband, which could be chocolate, cigarettes, lighters, alcohol, et cetera. Even in rehab, the "laws of the 'hood" applied.

Since I had no contraband, no one wanted to have anything to do with me, so I quickly became lonely. Sometimes God allows you to go through lonely times so that He can reveal himself to you and it is His way to protect you from the hand of the enemy. El Roi (which means "The God who sees" in Hebrew) was truly watching over me.

In rehab there is a protocol for doing things, which no one wanted to share with me right away. If the protocol wasn't followed, you were subject to "L.E. Time," which was "learning experience" time. L.E. Time was a form of punishment that you dreaded doing, but its purpose was to help you reflect on your mistakes, and correct them.

One of the procedures that was part of the facility's protocol involved wake-up time. At six o'clock each morning, the night person on watch would come into each room and yell, "Its time to wake up." Everyone would then get up, make their bed and place their shoes neatly under the bed. The room also had to be in pristine order.

After room check, everyone headed to the mess hall for breakfast. There, I was introduced to my big brother, who was supposed to show me the ropes. He wasn't much of a big brother because he tried to stay far away from me and didn't share any instructions with me.

Soon after breakfast, everyone gathered in the meeting hall for roll call. There was even protocol for how roll call was given. All the new folks had to sit in the front row, followed by the ones who were there a few months, and finally, those who had been there the longest.

The mission statement was recited from memory. Those who were new were expected to learn and recite the mission at a moment's notice from memory. If it were not recited correctly, the consequence would be L.E. Time. There was someone who was always assigned to speak at our meetings and they would tell stories from their past, both failures and progress. Sometimes I found it very boring, especially at the beginning.

You were also expected to have a job while you were staying at the facility. After the morning roll call and meeting, everyone went to their assigned jobs. I didn't have one, so one of the patients told me that I needed to go to the office to speak with my counselor. They told me that I couldn't just go into the office. I had to knock and wait until someone answered, then tell them who I was and why I was there.

It was awkward at first, like being in the military. "Julio Rubio, here sir."

"State your reason," I heard someone say from the office.

"I am new here, sir, and I wish to speak to my counselor." A few seconds later, I was greeted by this woman who they called Dorothy.

Dorothy seemed so friendly. She asked me how I was doing and how they were treating me. She knew why I was there but asked anyway. She asked about the medications I was taking. I was on many medications, each to treat one of the issues I was having. There was one "med" for anxiety, another for depression, others for diabetes, cravings, and nicotine, because I also smoked cigarettes.

She was interested in hearing my story of how I ended up as an alcoholic. She asked about my parents and family. I told her that my family didn't know that I was here and had given up on me a long time ago. It was then, for the first time, I broke down and cried.

Right away, my counselor began to set in motion the help that I needed. She arranged for me to receive a stipend so that I could get some new clothes and eyeglasses that were desperately needed. She also promised to help me get some official identification. I felt relieved. For the first time someone was going to help me. She assured me that, any time I needed anything, I should come to her.

The coordinator on duty was the one who would help you find a job on campus. After reviewing my file, he noticed that I was a successful chef. He was excited right away and said help was always needed in the kitchen.

There was a problem, however: All my passion and joy for cooking was no longer there. It was in the kitchen where my addiction to alcohol had manifested itself, so I had no desire to be in the kitchen again.

I reasoned with him, explaining why I did not want to work in the kitchen. The coordinator got very upset. The facility really needed help in the kitchen and being a chef was the only experience I had. He insisted that I give it a try. So, for about a week, I did so.

It was far from easy. Even making something simple such as oatmeal was a struggle for me, simply because I really didn't want to be there. Every fiber of my being resisted it because of its relationship for me to alcohol. The next week, I went to see my counselor. I told her that working in the kitchen was a trigger for me. Thankfully, she understood and immediately discontinued the assignment.

My next job was serving as an assistant in the facility office. There, I got to see many of the new patients coming into the program. Their faces were broken, shaken, and beaten down, so I felt glad inside when I watched them be transformed over time.

I didn't know it then, but El Roi was at work in what He allowed me to witness, as well as how I felt about the others I saw and got to know at rehab.

El Roi was also there when I saw my sister for the first time, during a day visit to my hometown, Yonkers, NY.

After three months working in the office, I was doing so well that I had become its coordinator. As the coordinator, I was allowed to make trips to pick up individuals who were coming into the program.

One particular day, I took a trip to Yonkers with a staffer named Henry. During our journey, Henry asked about my family. I told him they had turned their back on me and didn't even know where I was.

Henry suggested that I get in touch with them. I doubted they would listen to me if I tried, I told him, especially since I'd promised to change so many times before, but not followed through.

Knowing that we would be in my old neighborhood, however, made Henry press a little harder. He didn't want me to miss this opportunity to connect with family that I hadn't seen in years. I, on the other hand, was thinking about using the time to find someone to supply me with contraband, such as money or cigarettes.

We arrived at the outpatient center in Yonkers around 10:30 a.m. Our new clients wouldn't arrive until 4:00 p.m., so we had lots of time to spare. I told Henry I was going to walk around Getty Square downtown in search of cigarettes. Henry was cool about that. "Yes, go and get your smoke on."

As usual there was a lot of people walking on the sidewalk as I proceeded towards the Square. In the distance, I saw, from far away, someone who looked like my sister, Stephanie. This same person was looking at me also. She started walking towards me faster, and I did the same.

It *was* Stephanie! We were so excited to see each other. She asked where I had been. The family was worried and had been looking for me, she explained. They'd even tried searching in jails and hospitals. She was happy that I was getting help in a rehab center.

Now, while I was enjoying this happy reunion, I still had "getting cigarettes" on my mind, so I asked if she could buy me a pack. She refused, offering to get me coffee and a sandwich, if I wanted, but definitely no cigarettes. She then said she wanted to let the rest of the family know where I was so I gave her my contact information. Then we hugged and I started walking back towards the van.

I reflected on what had just happened. It had been great seeing my sister but what was I thinking, asking her for cigarettes? I felt convicted, and realized, then and there, that I needed to give up cigarettes, too. That was the last time I thought about or looked for cigarettes.

Henry was surprised to see me back at the van so early. I explained that I just saw my little sister. As he listened to me, tears were streaming down his cheeks. I didn't know it then but EL ROI was there, connecting me to my family.

El Roi continued watching over me as I continued this process of redemption on the road to recovery.

Psalm 139:1-6
"O Yahweh, you have examined me, and you know me. You alone know when I sit down and when I get up. You read my thoughts from far away. You watch me when I travel and when I rest. You are familiar with all my ways. Even before there is a single word on my tongue, you know all about it, Yahweh. You are all around me, in front of me and in back of me. You lay your hand on me. Such knowledge is beyond my grasp. It is so high I cannot reach it."

EL ROI MENU

Soup:
Fish Chowder

Salad:
Waldorf Salad

Fish Entree:
Spicy Cod

Meat Entree:
Chicken Piccata

Vegetarian Dish:
Vegetarian Baby Bok Choy

Dessert:
Sponge Cake

Prayer:

We Praise you Jehovah El Roi who watches over us. We are blessed coming in and we are blessed going out. We thank you for being here with us as we break bread together.
Amen

Fish Chowder
(Serves 8)

3 Tablespoons of organic Flax Seed Oil
3 cups of organic Vegetable Broth
3 cups of organic Seafood Broth
1 cup of organic Green Pepper cut into medium dice
1 cup of organic Red Pepper cut into medium dice
1 cup of organic Leeks cut into small dice
1 cup of organic Carrots cut into medium dice
1 cup of organic Onion cut into medium dice
½ cup of organic Lemon Grass finely chopped
2 pounds of organic of any Fish Filets cut into small piece
3 cloves of organic Garlic finely chopped
½ cups of organic kosher Non-Alcoholic White Wine
1 Tablespoon of organic all-purpose seasoning
1 Tablespoon of organic fresh Basil Leaves chopped
1 Tablespoon of organic Chive chopped
2 organic Bay Leaves
1 teaspoon of organic Black Pepper

1. In a 5-quart saucepan, heat oil over high heat. Add the celery, onions, carrots, green pepper, red pepper and leeks and lemon grass cook until they are tender then add the garlic until reach a brown color.
2. Add the fish to the pot and cook for 10 minutes. Add the white wine and the vegetable, seafood broth; bay leaves bring it to a boil keep cooking for 15 minutes.
3. Add the rest of the ingredients keep on cooking for 15 minutes serve.

Waldorf Salad

Waldorf Salad
(Serves 8)

8 cups of organic fresh Apples, medium diced
2 cups of organic Nuts, Chopped
1 cup of organic Celery, medium diced
1 cup of organic plain Greek yogurt
1 teaspoon of organic kosher Sea Salt
1 teaspoon of organic Black Pepper

1. Combine all ingredients in a large mixing bowl.
2. Mix well serve on 8 chilled salad plates, on a bed of organic Mix Greens.

Spicy Cod
(Serves 8)

8 (7 oz.) of fresh water Cod Fillets
4 cups of organic vegan Spicy Salsa (2- 8 ounce cans)
4 Tablespoons of organic fresh Italian Parsley, finely chopped
1 teaspoon of organic kosher Sea Salt
1 teaspoon of organic Black Pepper

1. Pre-heat oven to 375°F, place the fish fillets on a baked sheet tray. Sprinkle the fish with the spices and topped each fillets with the salsa.
2. Baked for 25 minutes and topped it off with the fresh parsley and serve.

Chicken Piccata
(Serves 8)

8 (7 oz.) organic Skinless Chicken Breast halves
4 Tablespoons of organic grated Pecorino Romano Cheese
1 cup of organic all-purpose Flour
1 teaspoon of organic kosher Sea Salt
1 teaspoon of organic Black Pepper
7 Tablespoons of organic raw Coconut Oil
5 Tablespoons unsalted organic Butter
1 cup of organic Chicken Broth
½ cup of organic Capers
½ cup of organic fresh Italian Parsley, finely chopped

1. Mix together the flour, salt, pepper and cheese. Coat the chicken cutlets well thoroughly in the flour mixture.
2. Heat the oil and 2 tablespoons of butter in a large skillet on medium heat. Add half of the chicken cutlets. Brown well on each side, about 5 minutes per side. Remove the chicken from the skillet and put it aside.

3. Add chicken stock, lemon juice and capers to the pan and reduce the sauce by half. Whisk the remaining butter and ingredients. Put the chicken on the plate and poured the sauce on top and serve.

Vegetarian Baby Bok Choy
(Serves 8)

2 cups of organic green onions, medium chopped
4 Tablespoons of organic Coconut Oil
6 organic Cloves of Garlic, finely chopped
2 pounds of organic Baby Bok Choy rinsed and trimmed and large cut
1 teaspoon of organic Sesame Oil
1 teaspoon of kosher Sea Salt
1 teaspoon of Black Pepper

1. Heat oil in a large roasting pan on high heat. Add onions then the garlic until nice golden brown, add the Boy Choy drizzle the sesame oil and the salt and black pepper. Cook for about 5 minutes.
2. Reduce the heat to low heat, stir and let it cook for 4 minutes and serve while is hot.

Sponge Cake
(Serves 8)

6 organic Eggs
1 cup of organic Brown Sugar
¼ teaspoon kosher Sea Salt
1 Tablespoon of organic fresh Lemon Zest
1 cup of organic Cake Flour
1 Tablespoon of fresh squeezed organic Lemon Juice

1. Beat eggs yolks until thick, add salt, sugar, lemon juice and lemon zest and mix well. Sift the flour. Fold into egg

mixture and fold in the egg whites that have been whipped until they hold their shape.

2. Pour into an oiled tube pan. Bake in slow oven for 325°F about 40 minutes. Add Blueberry or strawberry sauce on top and serve.

JEHOVAH SHAMMAH
God My Abiding Presence

Chapter Four

JEHOVAH SHAMMAH
God My Abiding Presence

> *Isaiah 43:1-2*
> *"Yahweh created Jacob and formed Israel. Now this is what Yahweh says: Do not be afraid, because I have reclaimed you. I have called you by name; you are mine. When you go through the sea, I am with you. When you go through rivers, they will not sweep you away. When you walk through fire, you will not be burned, and the flames will not harm you."*

"Julio Rubio, you have a phone call," I heard on the loud speaker. "Who could be calling me?" I wondered. I hardly ever got any phone calls. So I thought it had to be someone from the office or inside the facility. When I answered the phone, I was surprised to hear the voice of my brother, Marlon.

"Yo man! I have been looking for you! I am so happy to hear that you are in rehab and not a jail, hospital or the morgue."

We were so happy to connect finally after months of not seeing each other. Marlon was the closest to me of all my siblings. We came to the United States from El Salvador together and, through all the difficulties we faced during our childhood, we had developed a close bond.

Marlon wanted to come and see me right away. Usually in rehab, to get permission for family members to come for a visit, you had to make a formal request at least two weeks in advance. However, this was my first time during my six months in rehab that anyone wanted to come visit me.

I explained the rules to Marlon, that I needed to get permission from my counselor first, but that I would try. He said he'd ask if any other members of my family wanted to come, also.

That same day, I spoke to my counselor, asking her if my brother could visit me that very weekend. Though she reminded me that there were rules about such requests, she said she'd make an exception if she, herself, could be present. Of course, I agreed! I was so grateful that she was willing to do this for me. It was even on her day off!

I called my brother to tell him the good news. He surprised me by saying that my mother wanted to come, also. My other siblings weren't coming, but I didn't care. I was going to see Marlon.

Saturday arrived and I felt like a little kid in a candy store. I stood outside, watching and waiting for them to get there. I nearly jumped up and down when I saw their car pull up.

My brother and I embraced and started crying. Then they sat down and spoke to my counselor. I didn't know why they had to do it right away but, looking back, I see there was great wisdom in that.

They wanted to take me out to lunch, but my counselor said I wasn't ready for that. I started getting upset, but she made me realize that she had already made exceptions for me. She was firm in her decision, which again was wise, though I did not realize it at the time. We were allowed to have food delivered to the facility, but I could not leave the campus.

We decided to order some Chinese food and, though I was disappointed I couldn't go *out* to eat with them, I was still happy that my brother and mother had come to see me, and I was about to get some real food.

We didn't speak about how I had arrived at rehab, but about things that were going on in their lives. That was okay, because

I really didn't want to talk about me. I still felt shameful about the things I had done and wasn't ready to talk about the past.

They spoke about a Spanish church they were attending. They told me people there were praying for me, even when the family didn't know where I was. It was the same Spanish church I'd attended with bottles of liquor stashed in my coat pocket before I hit rock bottom. Now they were excited to share the news that I had been found and their prayers, ones I didn't even know were being uttered, were being answered.

Marlon asked me if I would be willing to come back to church once I finished rehab. I explained that soon I would be allowed to go off campus on overnight visits. We called them "twenty fours." On a twenty-four, I would be allowed to stay with family for twenty-four hours. I just had to request a visit. Marlon said that he would come and get me and I could stay overnight at my mom's. It was then that I would be able to visit the church.

The time of our visit was coming to an end, and I remember feeling a little sad. Part of me wanted to go with them. But before they left, Marlon gave me an IPod with sermons and Spanish and English worship music on it. (I didn't even know what an IPod was. He had to teach me how to use it.) Having an IPod was something that wasn't really accepted at the facility but, even in this, the Lord gave me favor, as my counselor gave me permission to keep it.

That night I couldn't wait to go to bed so I could listen to what was on my IPod. I was like a little kid with a new toy.

When I turned on the IPod that night, I saw there were videos on it, too. "How cool!" I thought. I clicked on a video and Bishop T.D. Jakes popped up. I had no idea who Bishop T.D. Jakes was, but the fact it was a video got my attention.

I started listening to his sermon. It was the first real sermon that I had ever heard. Amazingly, he spoke about rehabs. He said, " There are many rehabs out there, ones that are expensive, fancy ones for celebrities. But you can have all the rehab you want and none will ever work unless you have Jesus." That's when I knew what I really needed in my life: Jesus.

I never said a sinner's prayer because I didn't know I needed to do that. I just knew I needed and was willing to have Jesus in my life. Only if He were in my life would I truly and completely be free from alcohol and cigarettes, and get the fresh start in life I longed for. So I just said, simply, "Jesus, I need you." From that moment on everything changed. Jehovah Shammah (which means "God the Abiding Presence" or "The Lord is There" in Hebrew) came into my life that day and continued to be in my life from that moment on.

> *Exodus 33:14*
> *"Yahweh answered, My presence will go with you, and I will give you peace."*

JEHOVAH SHAMMAH MENU

Soup:
Pomegranate Gazpacho Soup

Salad:
Love Salad

Fish Entree:
Lemmon Mint Fillet of Sole

Meat Entree:
Shredded Beef

Vegetarian Dish:
Chickpea Stew

Dessert:
Rice Pudding

Prayer:

Thank you Jehovah Shammah, You are the God who knows all and sees all and you are the God who is abiding with us now. Make your presence known to each one who is at this table. Speak to us as we fellowship and bless this food as we eat together.
Amen

Pomegranate Gazpacho Soup

Pomegranate Gazpacho
(Serves 8)

4 cups of POM (Pomegranate) Juice
2 cups of organic European Seedless Cucumbers, cut into small dice
1 organic whole organic Red Onion cut into small diced
1 cup of organic bell Green Pepper cut into small dice
2 whole organic scallions cut into small dice
4 Tablespoons of organic Apple Cider
4 Tablespoons of organic Olive Oil
2 cloves of organic Garlic finely minced
½ teaspoon of organic Ground Cinnamon powder
½ teaspoon of organic kosher Sea Salt
½ Tablespoon of organic Seedless Jalapenos cut into small dice

1. Place all the ingredients in a large metal bowl mix it together well chill it for about an hour and served.

Love Salad
(Serves 8)

2 organic Mexican Avocados, thinly sliced
2 organic blood Oranges, sliced into 8 sections
1 pint of organic fresh Blueberries
1 pound of organic Mixed Greens
½ cup of organic Sugar
½ cup of organic Red Wine Vinegar
1 Tablespoon of organic Whole Grain Mustard
1 teaspoon of organic kosher Sea Salt
1 teaspoon of organic Black Pepper
2 Tablespoons of organic Onion Powder
1 cup of organic Vegetable Oil
1 Tablespoon of organic Poppy Seeds

1. Arrange the avocado, blood orange strawberries, blueberries and mix greens on 8 plates.
2. Blend remaining ingredients together in a blender and serve over salad.

Lemon Mint Fillet of Sole
(Serves 8)

8 (6 oz.) of fresh water fillets of Sole
8 Leaves of fresh Lemon Mint, finely chopped
1 Tablespoon of organic Paprika
1 ½ Tablespoons of organic raw Coconut oil
1 Tablespoon of organic fresh squeeze Lemon Juice
1 teaspoon of organic kosher Sea Salt
1 teaspoon of organic Black Pepper
½ cup of organic Non-Alcoholic White Wine

1. Preheat the oven to 350° F. Place fish fillets in a baking sheet tray.

2. Rub each fillets with coconut oil, sprinkle, salt, black pepper, paprika, Non-alcoholic white wine, lemon juice and the chopped lemon mint.
3. Baked for about 10 minutes or until desired doneness and serve hot.

Shredded Beef
(Serves 8)

3 pounds of organic Flank Steaks
3 large organic Spanish Onions cut into medium dice
3 organic Bell Green Pepper cut into medium dice
6 coves of organic minced Garlic
8 large organic Plum Tomatoes cut into large dice
3 organic Bay Leaves
2 teaspoons of organic kosher Sea Salt
1 teaspoon of organic Black Pepper

1. Boil meat with all the ingredients for about 2 hours until the meat is tender.
2. Strain let the meat cool down then shredded it as finely possible.
3. Puree the vegetable in a food processor.

Ingredients for the Sauce
3 large organic Spanish Onions cut into strips
2 large organic large Green Peppers cut into strips
6 organic cloves of Garlic minced
2 organic Bay Leaves
1 Tablespoon of organic Mexican Ground Cumin
4 Tablespoons of organic Olive Oil
2 cups of organic Non-Alcoholic Red Wine
1 teaspoon of organic kosher Sea Salt
1 Tablespoon of organic Black Pepper
1 16-ounce can of organic peas
1 16-ounce of organic Italian Roasted Red Peppers

1. Sauté onions and green pepper on oil until golden brown.
2. Add the rest of the ingredients and cook for 20 minutes.
3. Add shredded beef and puree vegetables. Stir well and cover and cook for 25 minutes over medium heat.
4. Garnish with peas and roasted red pepper strips and served.

Chickpea Stew
(Serves 8)

2 (16-ounce) cans of organic chickpea AKA Garbanzo Beans
4 Tablespoons of organic raw Coconut Oil
2 large organic Spanish Onions cut into medium dice
4 canned of organic Tomatillo green sauce
2 teaspoons of organic kosher Sea Salt
1 teaspoon of organic Black Pepper
2 teaspoons of organic ground Mexican Cumin
½ cup of organic chopped fresh Basil
2 teaspoons of organic ground Turmeric
1 can of organic Tomato Puree
4 cloves of organic Garlic finely chopped
2 cups of organic Vegetable Stock

1. Drain the chickpeas.
2. Sauté the onions and garlic in the oil in a large saucepan until golden brown.
3. Add all the spices and cook for about 4 minutes stirring constantly.
4. Add the chickpeas and 2 cups vegetables stock. Bring to a boil and simmer for 20 minutes, covered or until the chickpeas are soft.
5. Stir in the tomatillo and tomato sauce and fresh basil and cook for 4 minutes more and is ready to be served.

Rice Pudding
(Serves 8)

1 cup of organic short-grained Rice, uncooked
½ teaspoon of organic kosher Sea Salt
4 strips of organic Lemons
2 cups of Water
6 cups of organic Almond Milk
2 cups of organic Sugar
organic Cinnamon

1. Combine rice, water, salt and lemon strips. Bring to a boil.
2. Cook over low heat until rice is done (about 20 minutes).
3. Remove lemon strips. In a large heavy-bottomed saucepan, scald milk with cinnamon stick.
4. Add milk and cinnamon stick to cooked rice and cook over low heat, stirring with wooden spoon.
5. When mixture is creamy, add sugar and continue cooking and stirring for approximately 5 minutes.
6. Remove from heat. Remove cinnamon stick and the pudding should be creamy and not too thick it will thicken as it cools.
7. When ready to serve sprinkle with ground cinnamon.

RUACH QODESH
Holy Spirit

Chapter Five

RUACH QODESH
Holy Spirit

Joel 2:28–29
"After this, I will pour my Ruach on everyone. Your sons and daughters will prophesy. Your old men will dream dreams. Your young men will see visions. In those days I will pour my Ruach on servants, on both men and women."

As I continued to listen to the recorded messages, worship music and the Bible on my IPod, the Word of God was taking root inside of me in a way that caused a change to occur on the outside of me, as well. People in the rehab facility began to see me walk around with the Bible in my hand. Those who noticed the transformation started calling me "Bible boy."

I wanted to know more so I began seeking more. I found myself preaching to the walls and began to see myself talking to people. It was like the "fire shut up in my bones" that the prophet Jeremiah spoke about: "But if I say, I will not mention his word or speak anymore in his name, his word is in my heart like a fire, a fire shut up in my bones. I am weary of holding it in; indeed, I cannot." (Jeremiah 20:9)

I noticed that I wasn't feeling lonely anymore and the feelings of worry, fear and anxiety were slowly diminishing. The

Holy Spirit's presence was with me, making the necessary changes, and peace was there for the first time in my life. I had never experienced this peace before, and the urges for alcohol were gone. My focus was on what I was listening to and reading in the Bible. The fruit of the Spirit in Galatians 5:22-23 were becoming evident in my life: love, joy, peace, patience, kindness, goodness, faithfulness, gentleness and self-control were being cultivated and true transformation had begun. Things were starting to come together for me and I recalled the voice that spoke that day I wanted to end my life, telling me to "go get help." It was the voice of the Holy Spirit (the "Ruach Qodesh" in Hebrew) that saved my life. I was no longer looking for contraband or desiring wicked stuff. Now I was searching and looking for the things of God.

No one wanted to listen to me when I tried to talk to people about God in rehab. Group meetings there referred only to a higher power. However, a group didn't need to tell me to seek a higher power because I was getting to know the true and only living God, the only Higher Power there is.

My first "twenty-four," which was an overnight with my family, finally came. My brother came to pick me up on a Saturday. We were going to attend the Spanish church the next day.

Marlon said I needed to have a new outfit for church, so he took me shopping that day for some brand new clothes. That outfit became the only outfit I had for church or any other event. People seemed to look at me weird because I wore the same outfit over and over again. But that didn't matter to me. Before I had nothing suitable to wear for events; now I had one good outfit.

I didn't really know how to act when I started going to church. It was uncomfortable at first, and shame and condemnation would always be with me when I entered the doors. Sometimes the condemnation came from some of the church members. I especially felt it when they noticed that I was wearing the same outfit every Sunday.

The only place I felt comfortable sitting was in the back of the church in the very last row. Sitting there, I did the only thing I knew to do which was to pray and ask the Lord to speak to me. Shortly after praying that prayer, the Holy Spirit began to deposit words within me. Scripture references, which I did not know, would appear in my heart and when I looked up the reference, it would be a scripture verse that spoke directly to me. Psalms 23:1, "The Lord is my Shepherd, I shall not want," was one of them. No doubt about it. Remembering that the Lord was my shepherd was just the comfort I needed to get through the awkward transition I would soon be facing when I went from rehab to the outside world.

As I continued to go to that church, I would receive words of knowledge. I didn't know what they were at the time. I simply received these messages into my mind and heart and felt compelled to say them out loud.

At the end of each Sunday service, the pastor of the church would ask if anyone had something to share with the congregation from the Holy Spirit. I spoke out what was given to me from the Lord. It became very clear, however, that the people in the church didn't like what I was saying.

I asked my brother, Marlon, if I was saying something wrong. He would explain that I was saying exactly what needed to be said and he was amazed because I knew nothing of what was going on in the church.

I was so young in the Lord that I did not even know how to discern properly the words that I was receiving for the church. One particular word that I remember hearing from the Lord was that He was going to send a real angel to protect and save the church. What I did not know was that, a few weeks earlier, before I started going there, the pastor announced to the congregation that he was an angel that God sent to that church. So when I gave that word to the congregation, the pastor gave me this evil look. Ruach Qodesh began to unravel and reveal some of the hidden sins that needed to be dealt with in that church.

I continued to attend that church whenever I was able to get an overnight away from rehab. Ruach Qodesh, the Holy

Spirit, continued to work in my life at the church despite all that happened there. It was at that church that I learned to be sensitive to the Holy Spirit.

> *Psalms 51:10 "Create a clean heart in me, O Elohim, and renew a faithful spirit within me. Do not force me away from your presence, and do not take Ruach Qodesh from me. Restore the joy of your salvation to me and provide me with a spirit of willing obedience."*

RUACH QODESH MENU

Soup:
Mushroom Barley Soup

Salad:
Blue Cheese & Celery Cashew Salad

Fish Entree:
Balsamic Glazed Salmon

Meat Entree:
Venison Tips

Vegetarian Dish:
Lentil & Spinach

Dessert:
Date Pudding

Prayer:

We thank you Holy Spirit, Ruach Qodesh that you are among us today. We ask that you breath life in us and help us to be sensitive to your presence as we gather together around this table.
Amen

Mushroom Barley Soup
(Serves 8)

6 cups of organic Vegetables Broth
1 cup of thin sliced Portobello Mushroom
1 cup of organic Spanish Onions thinly sliced
4 cloves of organic Garlic, minced
1 cup of organic Celery thinly sliced
1 cup of organic Parsnip thin sliced
2 organic Bay Leaves
1-teaspoon fresh organic Thyme
1 Tablespoon of organic All Purpose seasoning
1 Tablespoon of organic Amino Liquid
½ cup organic pearled Barley
2 Tablespoons of organic Flaxseed Oil
1 teaspoon of organic kosher Sea Salt
1 teaspoon of organic kosher Black Pepper

1. In a medium soup pot heat the oil over medium high heat. Add the Portobello mushroom and onions and minced garlic, cook sauté until softened about 5 minutes.
2. Add the vegetable broth and carrots and celery, parsnip and the pearled barley and bring it to a boil. Reduce heat and simmer, uncovered for about 30 minutes add the thyme and rest of the ingredients and keep simmer for 5 minutes.

Blue Cheese and Celery Cashew Salad
(Serves 8)

1 cup of organic chopped roasted Cashew
1 cup of organic crumbled Blue Cheese
1 Tablespoon of organic Coconut Raw oil
3 Tablespoons organic Maple Syrup
½ of teaspoon of organic Cayenne Pepper
1 teaspoon of organic kosher Sea Salt
1 teaspoon of organic ground Black Pepper

2 bunch of organic Celery cleaned and discard the tops and cut into medium diced
8 cups of organic mix Italian salad
2 cups of organic Dried Cranberries
1 cup of organic Olive Oil
2 teaspoons of organic Lemon Zest
4 teaspoons of organic Lemon Juice

1. Keep the blue cheese at room temperature, add the coconut oil to a large skillet then add the cashew and toast them at low heat for a few minutes, continuously stirring. When the cashews are hot, turn off the heat and add maple syrup to the pan.
2. Add a pinch of cayenne to the glaze cashew remove from the stove and set them aside.
3. In a large metal bowl add the lemon zest, and lemon juice along with the salt and pepper. With a metal whisk stir in gradually the olive oil until smooth dressing consistency.
4. Take 8 salad bowls and equally arrange the Italian salad mix into the salad bowls, then drizzle the dressing upon each salad and topped with glaze cashew celery and dried cranberries and serve.

Balsamic Glazed Salmon

Balsamic Glazed Salmon
(Serves 8)

2 Tablespoons of organic Dijon Mustard
8 (6 oz.) of fresh water Salmon Fillets
1 cup of organic Green Onion, finely chopped
1 cup of organic Raw Honey
2 Tablespoons of organic Lemon Zest
1 teaspoon of organic Black Pepper
1 Tablespoon of organic Spanish Paprika

1. Preheat the oven at 350°F.
2. In a large bowl combine the following ingredients balsamic vinegar, Dijon mustard, honey, lemon zest, black pepper, paprika and green onions and whisk well together.
3. Add the Salmon fillets to the marinade and let it sit for about 2 hours.
4. Take Salmon fillets from the marinade and place them on a baking sheet tray.
5. And bake them for about 20 minutes or until they are done, place them in a nice plate and serve hot.

Venison Tips
(Serves 8)

2 pounds of Venison stew meat
1 large organic Spanish Onion cut into large dices
2 organic Green Peppers cut into large dices
2 organic Red Peppers cut into large dices
1 organic Yellow Pepper
2 cups of organic beef broth
1 cup of organic kosher Red Non-Alcoholic Wine
1 teaspoon of kosher Sea Salt
1 teaspoon of organic Black Pepper
1 Tablespoon of organic fresh Garlic finely chopped
½ cup of organic Coconut Oil
2 Tablespoons of organic Italian Parsley, roughly chopped

1. Heat the oil in a large frying pan, over medium high heat. Add the Venison chunks and cook until golden brown, then add the garlic and cook for about 3 minutes.
2. Add the Onions, Peppers, cook for about 5 minutes. Deglaze with Non-alcoholic red wine, when reduce add the beef broth and cook for about 10 minutes, add the salt and black pepper. Once the Venison is tender, turn the heat off and add the chopped Parsley and serve.
   * Beef or Lamb can be substituted for Venison

Lentil and Spinach
(Serves 8)

2 large organic Spanish Onions, slice into strips
2 Tablespoons of organic Garlic, minced
2 Tablespoons of organic Coconut oil
1 cup of organic green Lentils
4 cups water
2 pounds of organic fresh Baby Spinach
1 teaspoon of organic kosher Sea Salt
1 Tablespoon of organic Mexican Cumin
1 teaspoon of organic Black Pepper

1. Heat oil in a heavy roasting pan medium heat, sautéed onions for about 10 minutes until golden brown. Add minced garlic and cook for another 2 minutes.
2. Add the lentils and water to the pan bring it to a boil. Cover, lower the heat and simmer for about 30 minutes or until lentils are tender.
3. Add the spinach salt and cumin to the saucepan. Cover and simmer until all is heated about 15 minutes and black pepper and serve.

Date Pudding
(Serves 8)

3 organic Brown Eggs, well beaten
½ cup of organic Ground Suet
1 cup of organic Sugar
½ teaspoon organic kosher Sea Salt
½ teaspoon of organic Cinnamon
1 cup of organic Panko Breadcrumbs
1 pound of organic fresh Dates pitted and chopped
½ cup of organic sweet Soymilk
1 cup of organic chopped Nuts
1 teaspoon Baking Powder

1. Measure and combine baking powder, salt and cinnamon.
2. Combine eggs, suet, sugar breadcrumbs, Dates milk and nuts. Add dry ingredients mix thoroughly.
3. Place in a well oiled baking pan cover tightly and cook for 1 hour at 300°F or until the filling is firm and then chilled and serve.

JEHOVAH TSIDKENU
God My Righteousness

Chapter Six

JEHOVAH TSIDKENU
God My Righteousness

Psalms 23:3 "He renews my soul. He guides me along the paths of righteousness for the sake of his name."

It had been ten months since I first entered into rehab and now it was time to transition out into the "real world," so to speak. My time in the rehabilitation facility was coming to an end.

My counselor began to talk to me about going to a halfway house since I had no place to go. She explained to me that living at the halfway house would help me to transition back into society. She had worked it out so that I could still reside in Westchester County, near my family.

I was accepted into a halfway house in New Rochelle, NY, but I had to wait until a bed was available. During this time I began to get anxious about leaving rehab. It felt good to be moving on, yet scary at the same time. However, I liked the thought that I would be able to go and see my brother, Marlon, on a regular basis.

Finally, a bed became available at the New Rochelle halfway house and the date for my departure from rehab was set. On my last night in the facility, my counselor surprised me with a celebration party. It was one of the few times that I felt loved.

As we rejoiced together with food and a cake that she had made for me, people in my group wished me well and gave me hugs. I felt received and accepted for who I was and who I had become.

That last night they also had roll call, which would also be a sendoff for me. They called me up to the podium and announced that this was my last night. I shared with everyone the lessons that I had learned during my ten months in rehab.

As roll call ended, the group started pounding on the tables, starting from the back row and travelling down to the front row, shouting with hoots and hollering. The whole building exploded with applause, shouts and cheers. Thinking back on that day reminded me how it might have felt for Joshua and the Israelites when they marched around the walls of Jericho with a shout. The walls came down and there were victory. That last night at rehab was my victory shout!

The very next morning, Henry drove me to what would be my new home for the next few months. I entered rehab with a small hospital shopping bag, riding in a white van. Now I was leaving rehab with luggage, riding in a white van.

I settled into my new place with a big welcome from those who were living there. The first night, they served me a big meal, and then it was time to review all the rules. Every night I had to be in the house by 7:30 p.m. Each time I entered the home, I had to be tested for drugs or alcohol and, of course, I had responsibilities around the house. I still didn't want to cook, so when it was my turn to help in the kitchen, I just assisted and made small things. I still felt afraid to get back into cooking, as it was something that reminded me of my alcoholic days.

I continued to go to the Spanish church but, as time went on, I felt that there was something that wasn't right there. I did not feel the warmth and acceptance from the people there. The Lord continued to show me things, as I would look at people; I would see weird and sometime scary faces superimposed over their actual ones. Once I saw a person with a tail that was swaying back and forth. I didn't know what that all was about at the time, but later on, I learned that I was seeing demonic spirits.

My one year of sobriety was approaching, and I wanted to celebrate with the people at church. I ordered cake and had "The Lord Is My Shepherd" written on it. No one there seemed interested in my celebration. They treated me like an outcast. Even some of my family members who attended there would have little to do with me. The only person who seemed happy for me was my brother, Marlon.

Very few people would take a piece of the cake, either. The pastor's wife came up and pointed at the scripture on the top of it. "What is that?" she asked. I explained that it was Psalm 23. It wasn't the first time I'd experienced such a weird reaction to food I'd brought. Another time, the church was having a picnic and I brought a lot of food that day. No one would take my food. I remember I had to throw a lot of it away.

It was hard enduring this rejection but, despite the mistreatment I received, I still wanted to go to church, because my heart was so dedicated to God. It was because I sought Him that I went to services. I didn't go for the approval of any human being.

During this time when there seemed to be a lot of unrighteousness, Jehovah Tsidkenu, God my Righteousness, was showing me His righteous ways and placing in me a heart that would seek after Him.

I continued to do well at the halfway house. The holidays were coming up and I decided to go to my mother's for Thanksgiving. Marlon was living with my mom at the time, so I would get to see him, as well, along with other family members who were also coming to dinner.

Although she knew that I was an alcoholic and still going through outpatient rehab, my mother put all these alcoholic drinks on the table. She started talking about the drinks, swirling her cup around in front of me, smelling the alcohol close enough to me that I could smell it, too. It seemed like she was trying to set me up to fail, taunting me to take a drink. It made me feel so low and sick.

I left the dining room to go into the living room by myself and suddenly I wasn't hungry anymore. At that moment, I took a stand and said to myself, "I will not drink! I have come too far and one drink will ruin it for me." On the way home, Marlon stated he couldn't believe what our mom had done to me. It made me sick to think that my own mother would seek my destruction.

As the time drew closer for my discharge from the halfway house, it became clear to me that I could not live at my mother's house. My brother, Marlon, said that he would look for an apartment for us, where he and I could live together.

This decision forced me to look for a job sooner rather than later. A deli nearby was looking for someone to make sandwiches and run the grill. I decided to apply for the position. I still wasn't sure if cooking was the right job for me but, since I needed a job, I thought making sandwiches and hamburgers couldn't be all that bad. Nevertheless, when they asked if I could do the job, to make hamburgers and egg sandwiches, my doubts about working as a cook again made me unsure. "I think I can," I said timidly. They decided to give me a try.

The job paid $250.00 for a 60-hour workweek. This was my first job since rehab. I also had to sweep and mop the floors, and clean the bathroom, as well. This was a long way off from being a corporate chef in the Hilton, as I had been long ago, before alcohol had taken such a drastic hold on my life.

As I continued working for the deli, people began to notice how well I was doing on the job. They began to wonder if I had done this before. I was getting faster and faster with making sandwiches and hot foods, and I did it like a professional.

I started thinking that I should be making more money, considering all the work I was doing. People would give me compliments but, because I was making such a small salary, I became angry and resentful about cooking. Every time I filled an order, I did it with a terrible attitude.

One day one of the regulars came in and asked me to fix him an egg sandwich. Then he said, "You are a humble man, because this is not the first time you've done this kind of work. It's obvious that you have done this before."

The next day, as I was cooking, my attitude did not change. Then I heard the Lord say, "You are not doing this the right way. You have no idea how this sandwich could affect the one who is receiving it. A person could want to end their life, but when you make that sandwich with love, you are anointing that sandwich with My love. When you cook, you should cook with My love." From that moment on, I cooked with a different attitude. I was looking through different lenses. Jehovah Tsidkenu (Hebrew for "The Lord My Righteousness") was replacing my ways with His own. I was learning that I could do nothing without Him and everything through Him.

> *Psalms 71:19 "Your righteousness reaches to the heavens, O Elohim. You have done great things. O Elohim, who is like you?"*

JEHOVAH TSIDKENU MENU

Soup:
Black Bean Soup

Salad:
Jicama & Corn Salad

Fish Entree:
*Mahi Mahi
with Pineapple Salsa*

Meat Entree:
*Lamb Chops
with Chipotle Chili Butter*

Vegetarian Dish:
Spinach Pancakes

Dessert:
*Marsala Sabayon
with Berries Medley*

Prayer:

*Thank you Jehovah Tsidkenu, who is my righteousness. We ask
that you to come and show us your righteous ways as we eat
together. Be our righteousness as we fellowship around this table.
Amen*

Black Bean Soup
(Serves 8)

1 can of organic Black Beans
1½ Tablespoons of organic Flax seed Oil
1 whole of organic Spanish onion cut into small dice
1 cup of organic green Bell Pepper cut into small dice
4 cloves of organic Garlic minced
6 cups of organic Vegetable Broth
1½ cups of organic Carrots cut into small dice
1½ cups of organic Celery cut into small dice
2 organic Bay Leaves
1 Tablespoon of organic fresh Oregano finely chopped
1 Tablespoon of organic Ground Cumin
1 Tablespoon of organic Spanish Paprika
1 teaspoon of organic Cayenne Pepper

1. In a 5-quart saucepan heat the oil over medium high heat. Add the onions, bell peppers, and garlic cook stirring until softened about 3 minutes.
2. Add the vegetable broth and bring to a boil. Add the beans, carrots celery, bay leaves return to boil reduce heat and simmer 2 hour or until the beans are tender. Discard bay leaves kosher sea salt and organic black pepper to taste.

Jicama and Corn Salad
(Serves 8)

5 pound of organic Jicama, peeled and cut into medium dice
1 pound of sweet organic Corn Kernels
1 ½ Tablespoons of fresh squeeze organic Lime juice
2 teaspoons of fresh organic chopped Cilantro
½ teaspoon of any kind of organic Hot Sauce
1 teaspoon of organic kosher Sea salt
1 teaspoon of organic White Pepper

1. Combine the corn Jicama lime juice, cilantro and hot sauce in a bowl and toss. Add the sea salt and white pepper. Refrigerate for an hour then serve.

Mahi mahi with Pineapple Salsa
(Serves 8)

8 (6 ounce) fresh water Fillets
1 Tablespoon of organic fresh squeeze Lime juice
1 teaspoon of organic kosher Sea Salt
1 teaspoon of organic Black Pepper
1 Tablespoon of organic Coconut Oil

1. Take the fish steaks, sprinkle with lime juice and seasoning. Dip the fish into oil and allow any excess to drain away before placing on frying pan.
2. Place the Mahi Mahi presentation side down on the pan. Sautéed for about 3 minutes on each side.
3. When fish is opaque and firm, serve and topped it with the warm pineapple salsa.

Pineapple Salsa

2 pounds of fresh organic Pineapple cut into small dice
5 ounces of fresh organic Ploblano chilies finely chopped
1 teaspoon of fresh organic Jalapenos chilies finely chopped
1 ounce of fresh organic squeeze Lime juice
1 teaspoon of fresh organic Lime zest
1 ounce of organic Coconut Oil
3 teaspoons of fresh organic fresh Cilantro finely chopped
1 teaspoon of organic kosher Sea Salt
1 teaspoon of organic Black Pepper

1. Combine all ingredients, and let it sit for one hour before service.

Lamb Chops with Chipotle Chili Butter
(Serves 8)

8 (8 ounces) of Free-range Lamb chops
1 teaspoon of organic kosher Sea Salt
1 teaspoon of organic White Pepper
1 Tablespoon of fresh organic Garlic finely minced
1 cup of organic Coconut Oil
16 ounce of Chipotle Chili butter

1. Season the lamb chops with salt and pepper rub them with the coconut oil and garlic.
2. Place the lamb chops side down first on the grill or pan, cook undisturbed for about 2 minutes.
3. Turn the lamb chops over and complete cooking to the desired doneness about 2 to 4 minutes.
4. Before serving topped the lamb chops with chipotle chili butter.

Chipotle Chili Butter
(Serves 8)

1 pound unsalted Butter, room temperature
1 teaspoon of organic Chipotle Chili powder
½ teaspoon of organic Mexican Cumin
½ teaspoon of organic Garlic Powder
½ teaspoon of organic Onion Powder
organic Sea Salt and White Pepper to taste

1. Work the butter by hand until it is soft. Add the remaining ingredients and blend well. Add salt and pepper to taste.
2. The compound butter is ready to use now, or it may be rolled into a log put in the refrigerator and chilled for service.

Spinach Pancakes

Spinach Pancakes
(Serves 8)

2 pounds of fresh organic baby Spinach
1½ cups of organic Soymilk
3 organic brown eggs
4 ounces of organic all-purpose Flour
2 Tablespoons of organic Stevia Sugar
1 teaspoon of organic kosher Sea Salt
1 teaspoon of organic Black Pepper
1 teaspoon of organic Nutmeg
organic Coconut Oil for sautéed as needed

1. Blanch the spinach in boiling salted water or steaming for 1 minute.
2. Drain and rinse with cold water to stop the cooking. Drain and squeeze the spinach to dry it. Chop coarsely and reserve.

3. Combine the milk, butter eggs until evenly blended, stir together with the flour, pour in the milk mixture, and stir just until a smooth batter forms.
4. Combine the spinach with the batter and seasoning.
5. Heat a small amount of oil in a pan. Ladle 2 fl oz of batter into the hot pan for each pancake. Cook each pancake for about 2 minute on each side until golden brown serve immediately.

Marsala Sabayon with Berries Medley
(Serves 8)

10 ounces of organic Eggs Yolks
10 ounces of organic Stevia extract
7 ounces of organic kosher Non-Alcoholic Marsala wine
13 ounces of organic Heavy Cream
1 pint of fresh organic Mix Berries

1. Combine the eggs yolks, sugar, and non-alcoholic marsala wine in the bowl of an electric hand blender.
2. Whip over a hot-water bath until it reaches 180°F. Remove from the heat and transfer to the mixer. Whip until cool.
3. Fold in the whipped cream.
4. The sauce is ready to be served over the fresh berries medley.

My brother Marlon and I in Times Square NYC 2006 before
I became a believer.

My Out Patient Rehab Residence in NY

One of my "twenty-four's" Home Visit

Completion of my 2-year rehabilitation program

Following my true Master Chef at Harvest
Time Church. What a transformation!

My Brother Marlon

My friend David, myself and my brother Marlon at
Harvest Time Church.

Pastor Nick Uva at Harvest Time Church

Pastor Glenn and I at Harvest Time Church

Pastor Tommy Barnett and myself at the "Man Time" Conference in Stamford Connecticut

Engagement Photo of me and the soon to be Mrs. Rubio

April 27, 2012 - Our Wedding Day
Chef Julio & Emily Rubio

Mr. & Mrs. Julio Rubio
"Thank You Jehovah Nissi!"

My brother Marlon (my best man) and I on my Wedding Day

Getting ready to take my practical CEC Exam

Completing my practical CEC Exam

JEHOVAH JIREH
God My Provider

Chapter Seven

JEHOVAH JIREH
God My Provider

Philippians 4:19 "My God will richly fill your every need in a glorious way through Christ Yeshua."

y brother, Marlon, and I were able to secure an apartment in Yonkers, NY. We had to save every penny to do so, but we did it!

We continued going to the Spanish church, but there were a lot of rumors swirling around about the pastor having an affair and misappropriation of funds. People were leaving the church, but we were there to seek God so, despite all the rumors, we decided to stay. God would let us know when it was time to leave.

Not long after moving into our apartment, Marlon and the pastor had an argument. It got so heated that the pastor challenged Marlon to a fight, right outside the church. Marlon refused, so the pastor said he was no longer welcome in the church. Since Marlon was my only way to get to services, I had to leave, also. So we did.

Marlon wanted to go to another church right away, but I said "No, let's wait until God shows us a sign."

A week went by. Still God had not told us what to do. Marlon was getting anxious. "I feel like a fish out of water," he told me, "not going to services every week." I didn't want to simply go *anywhere*, though. I wanted to hear from God.

One Saturday, we decided to drive around our old stomping grounds in Yonkers. As we did, we started to reminisce about our childhood. We thought about our friend, David, and the bad things we used to do with him, such as drugs, alcohol, gambling and other stuff that I won't mention.

Just then, we heard some music on the street, so we parked our car and walked toward it. As we got closer, we realized it was a church group singing "Hosanna" so we decided to join in.

While we were clapping and singing, I noticed a gentleman from the church whispering to a couple of young girls and pointing to us. Suddenly the girls made a beeline toward us. They asked us if we wanted to visit their church and whether they could have our numbers. Marlon thought this might be the sign from God we'd been waiting for, but I didn't. Two young girls asking us to go to their church? Something didn't seem right to me. No, I decided, this wasn't God leading us.

It was a hot day, so Marlon suggested we get Italian ices at the supermarket before going back to our apartment. The way to our favorite store was blocked, forcing us to travel to another store on the other side of town. We didn't care, because we really wanted the Italian ices.

We walked into the store and who should we see but David! We were each surprised to see one another. "We were just talking about you," we exclaimed, "and remembering all the things we used to do."

"I don't do those things, anymore," David said, "because I've become a Christian!" Excited to learn this, we told him we were Christians, too. David was amazed.

He then told us about his church in Greenwich, CT, and upon learning that we were between churches, invited us to visit his. I wasn't sure. Greenwich was a pretty long drive from Yonkers.

Just then, Marlon pulled a flyer out of his pocket to show David. It advertised a Christian festival, "Bridgefest," that would soon be held in Ocean Grove, NJ. "The worship pastor from my church will be performing there," David said, pointing to the pastor's picture on the flyer.

I had never heard of a pastor performing in concert before. The concept seemed strange to me, but he had my attention. David suggested we come to his church that Wednesday evening. There would be a service and the worship pastor would be there. Something told me this was the sign from Jehovah Jireh that I had been looking for, so I told David we would go. I had no idea how many "effectual doors" were about to be opened for me, ones I didn't even dare dream were possible.

When we walked through the doors of Harvest Time Church that Wednesday night, Marlon and I were not prepared for what we would see. Compared to the little Spanish church that we had been attending, Harvest Time Church was huge! Not only big but also beautiful.

We stood in the foyer and just looked around. Our previous church didn't have a foyer that was nearly so grand. We then noticed a picture on the wall that showed drawings of their proposed new building. I looked at it for a while. Where was the kitchen? I couldn't find it but a church that big would surely have one!

We went inside the sanctuary. As worship began, both Marlon and I immediately felt this peace that we had never experienced in church. Our hands went up immediately towards heaven as we began to worship. I started to pray, loud enough for Marlon to hear: "Lord, I will be your chef here!" I don't know what made me say it. The words weren't even in my head before I heard them coming out of my mouth.

"What are you saying that for?" Marlon asked, bewildered.

"I don't know, it just came out," I replied.

We were so overwhelmed by the presence of God that we both moved toward the altar, in front of the church, fell on our knees and began to weep.

From that moment on, my life completely changed. Jehovah Jireh provided a church for us to attend. At Harvest Time Church I would begin to develop as a Christian. The gifts the Lord had given me would be stirred up and cultivated, and many doors of provision from my Heavenly Father would open up.

> *Matthew 6:31-33 "Don't ever worry and say, 'What are we going to eat?' or 'What are we going to drink?' or 'What are we going to wear?' Everyone is concerned about these things, and your heavenly Father certainly knows you need all of them. But first, be concerned about his kingdom and what has his approval. Then all these things will be provided for you."*

JEHOVAH JIREH MENU

Soup:
Red Lentil Soup

Salad:
Fruit Salad

Fish Entree*:*
Roasted Marlin

Meat Entree*:*
Seared Pork Chops

Vegetarian Dish*:*
Jerk Style Mushroom

Dessert*:*
Peaches in Red Wine

Prayer:

Thank you Father, Jehovah Jireh, who is our provider. Thank you for providing everything we need and thank you for every blessing that we have received.
Amen

Red Lentil Soup

Red Lentil Soup
(Serves 8)

2 Tablespoons of organic Coconut Raw Oil
1 cup of organic Red Lentil
1 cup of organic Celery, small diced
1 cup of organic Carrots mall diced
1 cup of organic Red Onions, small diced
1 cup of organic of organic Sweet Potatoes cut very small diced
10 cups of organic Vegetable Broth
1 Tablespoon of organic Cinnamon
1 Tablespoon of organic Spike Vegan Seasoning
1 teaspoon of organic Black Pepper
1 teaspoon of kosher Sea Salt
1 Tablespoon of organic Garlic Powder
1 Tablespoon of organic Smoked Paprika
½ cup of organic Italian Parsley chopped

1. In a 5-quart saucepan heat oil over high heat and add all
   vegetables and sweet potatoes. Cook for 10 minutes.

2. Add the lentil and vegetables broth bring it to a boil for about 20 minutes or until the lentil are tender.
3. Add the rest of the ingredients and cook for 10 minutes and serve.

Fruit Salad
(Serves 8)

8 cups of organic Arugula Greens
1 medium size organic Honeydew melon peeled, seeded and cut into bite size
1 small size organic Pineapple peeled and cut into bite-size
1 organic medium size Cantaloupe peeled and seeded and cut into bite-size
1 small size organic seedless Watermelon peeled and cut into bite-size
2 cups of organic fresh Green Grapes
2 cups of organic Red Grapes
½ cup of organic Balsamic Vinegar
½ of cup of organic raw Coconut oil
½ cup of organic fresh Mint chopped
1 teaspoons of organic kosher Sea Salt
1 teaspoon of organic Black Pepper

1. In a large mixing bowl combine all the ingredients mix well and chilled for about an hour in the refrigerator.
2. Take 8 Salad bowls and equally arrange the mixed greens and topped it with fruit salad mix and serve.

Roasted Marlin
(Serves 8)

8 (6oz) fresh Water Marlin Steaks
2 cups organic Raw Baby Shrimp
3 cups of organic Tomatoes small diced
1 cup of organic fresh Cilantro chopped
1 cup of organic kosher Non-Alcoholic White Wine
3 Tablespoons of organic Raw Coconut Oil

1 teaspoons organic Kosher Sea Salt
1 teaspoons of organic Black Pepper
1/2 cup of organic Shallot minced
½ cup of organic Garlic minced

1. In a large skillet at medium heat add the oil and when the oil is hot, add the fish, brown and cook each side for 3 minutes.
2. Deglaze the pan with non-alcoholic white wine with the fish still in the pan. Add butter garlic and the shallots, the shrimps and the tomatoes reduce for about 3 minutes at high heat.
3. Add the salt and pepper cook for another 4 minutes or until the fish is done.
4. Plate the fish topped it with the chopped cilantro.

Seared Pork Chops
(Serves 8)

8 (8oz) Pork Chops
1 cup of organic extra- virgin Olive Oil
½ cup of organic Balsamic Vinegar
3 Tablespoons of organic Dijon Mustard
½ cup of organic sweet Soy Sauce
½ cup kosher organic Non-Alcoholic Red Wine
2 Tablespoons of organic minced Garlic
1 teaspoon of organic kosher Sea Salt
1 teaspoon of organic Black Pepper
2 Tablespoons of organic fresh Rosemary chopped
2 Tablespoons of organic fresh Italian Parley

1. Place the pork chops in a mixing bowl add all ingredients and rub the steaks well, marinade then for 2 hours in the refrigerator.
2. In a large frying pan on high heat take the chops and seared each chops for about 7 minutes on each side or until they are done and serve.

Jerk Style Mushroom
(Serves 8)

2 organic medium size Spanish onions cut into medium chunks
4 organic Plum Tomatoes cut into medium chunks
8 large organic Portobello Mushroom Caps clean and cut into medium chunks
2 organic Red Pepper clean and cut into medium chunks
1 cup of organic raw Coconut Oil
1 cup of organic kosher Non-Alcoholic White Wine
1 teaspoon of organic kosher Sea Salt
2 Tablespoons of organic Jamaican Jerk seasoning

1. Heat the oil in large frying pan over high heat. Sauté the onions, peppers, tomatoes and mushroom cook for about 12 minutes then deglaze with the wine and reduce for about 2 minutes.
2. Add the rest of ingredients and cook until golden brown and serve hot.

Peaches in Red Wine
(Serves 8)

8 whole ripe Organic Peaches, peeled, pitted and sliced
6 Tablespoons of organic Stevia Powder Sugar
2 Tablespoons of fresh organic chopped Mint
1 bottle of organic kosher Non-Alcoholic Red Wine

1. Place the peaches and all the ingredients in a mixing bowl mix well using a rubber spatula let stand for at least 2 hours.
2. In 8 Martini glasses fill each one with the mix peaches and serve.

GO'EL
My Redeemer & Defender

Chapter Eight

GO'EL
The Lord My Redeemer & Defender

Job 19:25 "But I know that my Go'el lives, and after-wards, he will rise on the earth."

Soon after we started attending Harvest Time Church, there was a reception for those who were new to the church. David told Marlon and myself that we should go to it. We'd never attended a newcomer's reception before, so we were very excited about going.

When the day for the reception arrived, Marlon and I were the first ones to get there, so we just hung out, having some snacks that were laid out on a table in the church prayer room.

Soon, some pastors entered the room, introducing themselves to us, one by one. One of first was Pastor Glenn Harvison. He was the Senior Pastor. He asked us where we were from. As we continued talking to him, a question began burning in my heart that I knew I wanted to ask him.

Over the years, I would always reach out to my mother for acceptance and love; I never got it, however. Instead she would act, many times, in ways that would hurt me and cause me to feel defeated. I wanted to honor my parents, but did that always mean taking blows that were hurtful and demeaning to me? Perhaps Pastor Glenn would have the answer.

"What should I do, Pastor Glenn, if every time I go to my mother, she keeps shutting the door in my face? Do I still have to keep honoring her?"

"Well the Bible does say to honor your parents," Pastor Glenn responded, "but that doesn't mean you have to be a doormat." From that moment on, I decided that I would help my mother when she needed it. I would be respectful, but I would not allow her to hurt me any more.

A few weeks later there was an announcement regarding an upcoming class for those who were interested in becoming members of the church. Both Marlon and I felt that this was the thing to do, so we signed up. We'd never attended a membership class before so we were not sure if we needed to bring anything. It was a class, so we assumed we would likely be expected to take some notes.

Again we were the first ones to arrive for the class. Pastor Glenn and a couple of other people came into the classroom. They were expecting a few more people, so we were all just sitting there, waiting. I decided to use the time to ask about a kitchen in the new building. "When I looked at the architect's drawings posted in the foyer," I said to Pastor Glenn, "I didn't see a kitchen anywhere." Pastor Glenn explained that the Greenwich zoning laws were very complicated and made building a commercial kitchen difficult and expensive.

I decided to be bold: "Well, I see a big kitchen here with cameras and lights, and I think I am going to do a cooking show from here."

From the corner of my eye, I could see that Marlon wanted to crawl underneath the table. Another guy, who reminded me of Tommy Hilfiger, started laughing.

Even Pastor Glenn giggled. "No I don't think so," he responded. Yet something inside me kept wanted to press on. "We serve a King, and He can supply us anything!" I insisted. Still, Pastor Glenn replied, "I don't think that's going to happen."

Feeling a little crushed, I stopped pursuing the idea, even though, deep down in my heart, I still believed God could do what I envisioned He would.

Once the office staff learned that I was a chef, they all wanted me to join the Hospitality Ministry of the church. They were having a meeting, so I decided to attend. I was the only man there, but they were all happy to see me. What a blessing I would be, they all agreed.

Not long afterward, I was making fruit platters, cheese platters, crudités and other dishes for the newcomer receptions and membership classes. I felt redeemed! The very thing that I thought I couldn't do anymore because it was associated to my addiction – be a chef – was now the very thing God was resurrecting and using to bless others! I was so grateful!

Not only did God open doors for me to use my talents and skills for my church, but He started giving me favor with people in the marketplace, as well. I started being hired as a private chef for various events in the region. One event, a local wedding, was even featured on the TLC program, "Four Weddings." I was amazed at what God had done, taking a talent the enemy had used to bring about such evil in my life, and turning it into something to bring Him glory.

Soon after the TLC program aired, Harvest Time Church asked if I would be willing to host a breakfast at their satellite campus for its upcoming anniversary. They would be doing a big promotion for it, the church staff explained, and would do a big plug for me.

I'll never forget the first Sunday that the anniversary breakfast was announced at church. Pastor Glenn called me "Chef Julio Rubio." Then he said, "With a name like Chef Julio Rubio, don't you think that he should have his own TV show?"

From that moment on, Pastor Glenn started referring to me as "Celebrity Chef Julio Rubio," and Go'el, my Redeemer, was there every time, defending the very passion and gifts He had placed within me, those the enemy had tried to strip from my life forever. The lie I'd believed for years – the one that told me I would never be a chef again; that I didn't have the talents to do it and never would; that going back to doing the work I loved best would only bring misery, addiction and defeat – was being erased, as Go'el took what the enemy meant for my destruction and turned it into life, not just for me, but for others, too!

You see God wasn't only using my food, but my talents, as well. One weekend, our church had a missions conference, and I was put in charge of the International Dinner. Donning my chef coat and hat, I recruited volunteers to make assorted international dishes, and even donated my chef's services as one of the items for the weekend missions auction. My item alone raised over $1000.00 for His Kingdom's sake. God was using my talents as a chef to bring the Gospel to the world!

Don't ever think that you can be stripped of the passions and gifts that God has given you. Go'el will defend and redeem back everything that the enemy has tried to destroy!

Psalms 19:14 "May the words from my mouth and the thoughts from my heart be acceptable to you, O Yahweh, my rock and my Go'el."

GO'EL MENU

Soup:
Split Pea & Turkey Soup

Salad:
Cabbage Pineapple Salad

Fish Entree:
Baked Salmon Cakes

Meat Entree:
Fried Chicken

Vegetarian Dish:
Vegetable Frittata Roasted Potato

Dessert:
Carrot Pie

Prayer:

We praise you oh Lord who bears the name of Go'el. You name is victorious and we bring honor to the one who defends and who will fight for us. So we gather together around this table to speak about your mighty acts and how you have saved us from our enemies.
Amen

Split Pea & Turkey Soup
(Serves 8)

4 cups of organic Turkey Stock
4 cups of organic Vegetable Broth
1 Tablespoons of organic raw Coconut Oil
6 cloves of organic Garlic, minced
10 ounces lean organic smoked Turkey Breast finely diced
2 organic Bay Leaves
3 teaspoons of Chopped fresh organic Thyme
3 teaspoons of chopped fresh organic Marjoram
2 Tablespoons of organic Amino Liquid
1 cup of organic Spanish onion medium diced
1 cup of organic Celery medium diced
1 cup of organic Carrots medium diced
1 teaspoon of organic kosher Sea Salt
1 teaspoon of organic Black Pepper
2 Tablespoons or organic Parsley

1. Rinse the peas under cold water in a medium soup pot place the peas and vegetables broth and the turkey broth boil the peas for 25 minutes until they are tender.
2. In a separate pan in a medium heat add the oil, sauté the onions, celery, and carrots for about 7 minutes. Put the vegetables back into the soup pot with the peas and broth. Add the rest of the ingredients bring it to a boil for 10 minutes turn off the soup and served.

Cabbage Pineapple Salad
(Serves 8)

6 cups of organic Iceberg lettuce
6 cups organic shredded Cabbage
2 cup of organic fresh Pineapple, cut into medium chunks
1/3 cup of organic Pineapple juice
2 Tablespoons of organic Coconut oil

3 Tablespoons of organic plain Yogurt
1 teaspoon of organic kosher Sea Salt
½ teaspoon of organic Black Pepper

1. Combine all ingredients in a large mixings bowl and mix well,
   and serve on a bed of iceberg lettuce on 8 chilled salad plates.

Baked Salmon Cakes
(Serves 16 cakes)

4 organic Brown Eggs, lightly beating
1 teaspoon of organic kosher Sea Salt
1 Tablespoon of organic Italian Seasoning
2 pounds of fresh water organic cooked Salmon
1 large organic Red Bell Pepper, cut into small dice
1 large organic Green Bell Pepper, cut into small dice
1 Large organic Red Onion, cut into small dice
1 teaspoon of organic Black Pepper
4 organic Green Onions, cut into small dice
1 Tablespoon of organic fresh squeeze Lemon Juice
2 cups of organic Japanese Bread Crumbs (Panko)

1. In a large bowl put all the ingredients and mix well.
2. Form each cake into 4-ounce patties and place then in a
   large sheet pan with parchment paper.
3. Baked salmon cake at 350°F for 20 minutes each side or
   until golden brown and serve.

Fried Chicken
(Serves 8)

10 pounds of organic 8 cut fryer Chicken parts
4 cups of organic Greek Yogurt
2 large of organic Spanish Onions, cut into sliced

½ of cup of organic fresh Herb mix (Parsley, Lemon Thyme, chives)
1 teaspoon of organic Smoked Sweet Paprika
2 teaspoons of organic Cayenne Pepper
4 cups of organic all- purpose Flour
1 teaspoon of organic Garlic Powder
1 teaspoon of organic Onion Powder
1 teaspoon of organic kosher Sea Salt
1 teaspoon of organic Black Pepper
4 cups of Canola oil or Peanut oil

1. Soak the chicken for 8 hours in yogurt with onions, herbs, paprika, and cayenne pepper.
2. In a colander drain the chicken leaving the herbs on the chicken. In a large bowl mix the flour with the seasonings, add the chicken to the flour mix and coated the pieces well.
3. In a large heavy-bottomed skillet or cast iron add the oil, using a oil temperature Thermometer check the oil when reaches 325°F add the chicken and cook for 20 minutes or reaches 165°F internally. Using tongs to remove the chicken from the oil place it on paper towel to drain the excess oil then ready to be served.

Vegetable Frittata with Roasted Potato
(Serves 8)

2 pounds of organic Baby Red Potatoes, cut into small dice
4 cloves of organic Garlic finely minced
4 Tablespoons of organic Coconut Oil
16 organic brown Eggs, lightly beaten
1 cup of organic Sour Cream
1 small organic red onion, medium dice
1 pound of organic Baby Spinach
1 cup of organic Roasted Red Peppers
2 cups of organic Parmesan Cheese
1 teaspoon of organic Black Pepper

1. Preheat oven to 400°F and on a baking sheet tray layer the potatoes. Drizzle 1 Tablespoon of oil, salt and pepper and cook for 25 minutes.
2. In a medium bowl whisk together eggs and sour cream and the entire remaining ingredients, include the cooked potatoes. Transfer the mix to a 2-inch banking pan, and cook for 30 minutes at 325°F or until firm. Cut into squares and serve.

Carrot Pie
(Serves 8)

1 (9-inch) frozen Pie Shell
1 cup of organic cooked shredded Carrots
½ cups of organic Brown Sugar
2 cup of organic Soymilk
3 organic brown Eggs, well beaten
½ teaspoon of organic Cinnamon
½ teaspoon of organic fresh Ginger
¼ teaspoon of organic kosher Sea Salt
4 Tablespoons of Butter

1. Sautéed shredded carrots in butter until golden brown.
2. Combine all the ingredients and pour into a ready cooked pie shell.
3. Bake at 425°F until crust is brown and filling is firm.

Carrot Pie

JEHOVAH TSUR
The Lord My Rock

Chapter Nine

JEHOVAH TSUR
The Lord My Rock

Psalms 95:1"Come, let's sing joyfully to Yahweh. Let's shout happily to the rock of our salvation."

One Sunday at the end of service, a few weeks after Marlon and I had begun attending Harvest Time, Pastor Glenn asked those who wanted to give their lives to Christ to raise their hands. I responded, following him as he asked us to stand and repeat a prayer after him. It was a prayer for salvation, the first one I'd ever prayed in my life.

Now, I believe Jesus came into my life that night in rehab when I admitted my need for Him, but this was the first time I had publicly confessed my faith and trust in Him. As I did so, I understood for the first time that, if there were any pride still left within me, that pride had to bow to the name of Jesus then and there! He had to be first. All that exalted me, or put me first in any way, had to go!

Over the next weeks and months, I watched as the Lord began building my faith. My foundation in Christ grew strong, both through Sunday services and midweek classes offered at Harvest Time. (I loved going to church so much that I would go whenever possible.)

One of the classes I attended was called "Cleansing Streams." Held over a period of several weeks, it helped you deal with any negative behaviors or attitudes that had a strong hold over you and your family repeatedly for generations or past wounds that might have occurred through your family line.

The class also included a weekend retreat where issues of the heart were revealed. During rehab, they just skimmed the surface of dealing with family issues. At the retreat, however, the Lord began to do what I'd call "heart surgery" concerning those issues. For the first time, I learned I had to forgive myself as well as family members. I also learned that my Heavenly Father could father me and stand in place of the biological father I never knew.

It was during this retreat that I heard the word "condemnation" for the first time and learned what it really meant. "Condemnation is the accusing voice of the enemy telling us how bad we have been and how unworthy we are," Pastor Chris Hayward, President of Cleansing Stream and leader of the retreat, taught us. "Condemnation, which comes from Satan, is intended to push us down and to make us feel defeated and unworthy of God's love, grace and acceptance." Boy, did I know what he was talking about! Addicts feel condemnation all the time.

Fortunately, Pastor Chris and the rest of the ministry team didn't stop there. They told us there was hope. Through Jesus Christ, we had been made free. "Therefore, there is now no condemnation for those who are in Christ Jesus." (Romans 8:1)

Knowing this truth really helped. Now, whenever I started to feel condemned by my alcoholic past, I would remember that scripture and say it out loud to myself. "I don't need to feel condemned. My Heavenly Father has set me free!" *[If you'd like to learn more about Cleansing Stream and perhaps find a class near you, please visit their website: www.cleansingstream.org]*

A little while after the Cleansing Stream retreat and class were finished, the church announced that it was having a water baptism. I had been baptized before, but I hadn't understood what it meant at that time. So I decided to do it now, again, as another public confession that Jesus Christ was truly my Lord and King. Being immersed in water signified that I was cleansed of my old life and now I had a new life in Jesus Christ. The more steps I took to acknowledge and profess my faith, the freer I felt.

Jesus Christ took away my addiction, but now He was working from the inside out to make me completely new. Participating in rehabilitation programs were helpful, but only Jesus Christ could really, fully set you completely free.

Jesus once told a story about a man who built his house on a rock:

> *"I will show you what everyone who comes to me, hears what I say, and obeys it is like. He is like a person who dug down to bedrock to lay the foundation of his home. When a flood came, the floodwaters pushed against that house. But the house couldn't be washed away because it had a good foundation. The person who hears what I say but doesn't obey it is like someone who built a house on the ground without any foundation. The floodwaters pushed against it, and that house quickly collapsed and was destroyed."* (Luke 6:47-49)

While I was going to church and taking the classes, Jehovah Tsur was the rock on which my foundation was being built. Sadly, not all people who are seeking freedom from their addictions go to the Rock. Others do, but then quit right there, rather than putting in the additional work needed to establish a proper foundation on that Rock. Some people wander aimlessly, hopping from one church to another, and their foundation never takes root or shape. They are not firmly grounded in the Word of God. Then, when the storms of life come, they are not able to overcome them, but sadly turn back to their addiction.

I am so grateful that I was led to a church in which a strong foundation could be built on the Word of God and trust in Christ. Only in Him can the strength you need to survive the storms of life be found. There is no other Rock than Jesus.

Isaiah 26:3-4 "With perfect peace you will protect those whose minds cannot be changed, because they trust you. Trust Yahweh always, because Yah, Yahweh alone, is an everlasting rock."

JEHOVAH TSUR MENU

Soup:
French Onion Soup

Salad:
Asparagus Artichoke Salad

Fish Entree:
Sautéed Orange Roughy

Meat Entree:
Grilled Chipotle Chicken

Vegetarian Dish:
Quinoa with Black Beans

Dessert:
Black Walnut Pie

Prayer:

*We thank you Jehovah Tsur that you are my Rock that we can
depend on. We praise you for your word and your promises that
they are yes and amen. We ask that you come and abide
with us as our special guest as we break bread together.
Amen*

French Onion Soup
(Serves 8)

10 cups of organic Vegetable Broth
2 pounds organic Spanish Onions, thinly Sliced half moon
1 Tablespoon of raw Stevia Sugar
6 cloves of organic, minced
4 teaspoons of organic Cornstarch
½ cup of organic kosher Non-Alcoholic White Wine
2 organic bay leaves
3 teaspoons of organic fresh Thyme
2 Tablespoons organic All-Purpose Seasoning
2 Tablespoons of organic Amino Liquid
5 Tablespoons of organic Coconut Oil
8 slices of organic fresh Bread
2 Tablespoons of organic fresh Parsley finely minced
12 ounces of grated organic Parmesan Cheese
2 Tablespoons of organic Cumin
2 Tablespoons of organic ground Onion Powder

1. Thinly sliced the onions. Heat the oil in a large soup pot, medium-low heat, add the onions and sauté for 10 minutes or until they are beginning to turn brown. Add the minced garlic, sugar and chopped thyme, turn the heat down and cook, stirring occasionally for 30 minutes, or until the onions are caramelized golden brown.
2. Add the cornstarch and cook stirring constantly, for 2 minutes. Add the non-alcoholic wine, gradually stir the vegetable broth and bring it to a boil, skimming off the foam that rises to the surface, then reduce the heat and simmer for about 40 minutes.
3. Meanwhile, preheat the broiler to low to medium heat. Toast the bread on both sides under the broiler, and then sprinkle the cheese on one side of the toast.
4. Ladle the soup into 8 ovenproof bowls and set on a banking sheet. Place each piece of toast in each bowl, place under the broiler for about 1 minutes until the cheese is melted and served immediately.

Asparagus Artichoke Salad
(Serves 8)

2 pounds of fresh thick organic Asparagus, ends broken off
and cut into medium cut
1 large Red Onion, cut into thinly strips
3 Tablespoons of fresh organic Lemon Juice
1 pint of organic Grape Tomatoes cut in half
2 (15-ounce) organic cans of marinated Artichoke Hearts cut
into quarter
1 teaspoon of organic Sea Salt
1 teaspoon of organic Black Pepper
1 Tablespoon of organic minced Garlic
2 Tablespoons of organic Olive Oil

1. Roast the asparagus at 400°F coat the asparagus spears
   with 1 Tablespoon oil and salt and pepper for about 10
   minutes or tender.
2. Remove the asparagus from the oven and cut.
3. Put the asparagus with the remaining ingredients in a large
   bowl and mix well serve and chilled.

Sautéed Orange Roughy
(Serves 8)

8 (7 ounce) fresh water orange Roughy
1 cup of organic Orange Juice
2 Tablespoons of organic raw Coconut Oil
1/3 cup of fresh organic Lemon Juice
1 teaspoon of organic Black Pepper
1 teaspoon of organic kosher Sea Salt
1 teaspoon of organic Lemon Pepper Seasoning

1. In a large mixing bowl put the fish fillets into the bowl and
   add the orange juice and lemon juice and the rest of the
   ingredients let it marinade for about 2 hours.

2. In a large skillet on medium heat add the oil and place the fish and cook for about 4 minutes on each side or until the fish is flaky and serve.

Grilled Chipotle Chicken

Grilled Chipotle Chicken Breast
(Serves 8)

8 (8oz) organic skinless boneless Chicken breast
1 Tablespoon of organic Chipotle Powder
1 Tablespoon of organic Paprika
3 Tablespoons of organic Garlic Powder
1 teaspoons of organic kosher Sea Salt
2 Tablespoons of organic Onion Powder
2 Tablespoons of organic fresh Thyme, finely chopped
2 Tablespoons of organic Ground Cayenne

2 teaspoons of organic Black Pepper

1. In a medium bowl, mix together the herbs and spices for later use.
2. Pre-heat the grill for medium- high heat. Rub some of the seasoning mix to both sides of the chicken. Lightly oil the grill grates place chicken on the grill and cook for 7 to 8 minutes on each side until the juices are clear and serve.

Quinoa with Black Beans
(Serves 8)

2 cups of organic cooked Quinoa
3 Tablespoons of organic Coconut Oil
2 organic Spanish Onions cut into small dice
2 organic Red Bell Peppers, cut into small dice
1 teaspoon of organic Black Pepper
1 teaspoon of organic Kosher Sea Salt
1 Tablespoons of organic Chili Powder
2 small cans of organic Black Beans
2 small cans of organic diced Tomatoes
1 Tablespoons of organic Garlic finely chopped
2 cups of organic Vegetables Broth

1. In a large pot heat the oil over medium heat, cook the onions, bell pepper, garlic and cook until tender about 5 minutes.
2. Stir in the chili powder, salt and black pepper the tomatoes and the black beans and the vegetables stock covered and stirring for about 20 minutes add the quinoa and serve.

Black Walnut Pie
(Serves 8)

1 (9-inch) frozen pie shell
1 cup of organic Brown Sugar

2 organic Brown Eggs
½ cup organic Chopped Nuts
1/8 teaspoon kosher Sea Salt
1 ½ cups of organic almond Soy Milk, scalded
3 Tablespoons of organic Cornstarch
1 teaspoon of organic Vanilla flavor extract
1 Tablespoon of organic, melted Butter

1. Combine sugar, butter, cornstarch, and salt. Add milk slowly, stirring constantly.
2. Cook over hot water until thick and smooth.
3. Separate the eggs, beat the eggs yolks and slightly add to the mixture. Cook for 1 minute then add the nuts and vanilla extract.
4. Fold beaten eggs whites. Pour into baked pie shell.
5. Baked in the oven at 350°F degree until the filling is firm.

JEHOVAH NISSI
The Lord My Banner

Chapter Ten

JEHOVAH NISSI
The Lord My Banner

Song of Songs 2:4
"He has taken me to the banquet hall, and his banner
over me is love."(NIV)

*A*fter attending Harvest Time Church for a few months, I was getting to know some of the people there. I had never felt such warmth and love in any church before!

One of the ushers, Sal, would always greet my brother and I with a warm smile and took the time to know us, as well. One Sunday, he invited us to dinner at his house after church. We happily accepted his warm invitation. Such offers didn't come to us very often.

When we arrived at Sal's house, we noticed other people from Harvest Time were there, as well. Sal introduced all of them to us, but the one that stood out in my mind was Emily.

I'd noticed Emily before. She was part of the Harvest Time worship team, and would often sing with the team during Sunday service. She also tended to sit near the pastors in the front row, so I assumed she must also be a pastor. Beyond that, she was beautiful. Still, I didn't think much about it. I assumed she was married.

As the evening wore on, I talked to many of the people I met but, for some reason, not once did I have a conversation with Emily. In fact, I wouldn't meet her again until a few months later, during the holiday season. Of course, I'd see her singing in church on Sunday, but, for whatever reason, we never talked.

Then, one Sunday after Thanksgiving, Emily spotted Marlon and I after service. "Hey, I am having a Christmas party at my house. Would you like to come?" We nodded with excitement. Then I mentioned I was a chef and would be happy to bring a dish. She seemed glad for the offer and said she would send us her address and directions by e-mail.

But, for whatever reason, I never heard from Emily. Finally, on the day of the party, I told Marlon, "If I don't hear from her in a few minutes, I guess we won't be going." I needed to know soon, if I was going to have enough time to shop for the items to make my baked ziti. About ten minutes later, my phone buzzed. There was an e-mail from Emily. "I guess we're going," I said to Marlon, beaming. "Let's go shopping."

Marlon and I had never seen a neighborhood as nice as the one Emily lived in. It was like no place we had ever seen before. Once we pulled up, however, we immediately recognized other members of the church walking into her house. We knew we would have fun, and it was great getting to know them.

"Wow! What a huge deck!" I said to Emily, in admiration of the way her house was arranged for a nice outdoor party. "I could see myself grilling some steaks out here." She usually had a number of barbecues during the summer, she answered, so she would make sure to invite us to one.

That's when we happened to notice the large moon floating in the sky above us. We took a moment to look at it, then went inside, where Emily busied herself with picking up garbage from the tables and cleaning.

"Have you ever been married before?" I asked her, as I watched her bustle about the room.

When she said she had not, I was very surprised. "Wow, you are so beautiful," was all I could reply. She thanked me.

Then I added, "Well, I tell you one thing, you won't be single for long!"

" Thank you Julio. That was sweet."

I kept looking at her as she continued cleaning. I almost got the courage to ask her out, but then one of the other guests came in and interrupted our conversation. The opportunity never came again that evening.

It wasn't until after Christmas that I was able to talk with Emily again. I was home hanging out with Marlon when I got enough courage to ask if I could borrow his computer. I didn't have a computer and Marlon was very particular about his. To my surprise, he said yes.

I went on Facebook and discovered that Emily was online, then, too. Here was my chance to connect with her. We started chatting and shortly after, I found myself asking her to have coffee with me. (It was easier to ask her on Facebook than in person, as it is easier to get turned down on the computer than face to face.)

"Would you be interested in going out for coffee with me?" was what I typed in the chat box.

"Sure!" was the response.

"Really?" I said.

"Yes," she typed back.

"Wow, I can't believe it," I responded.

"Why?" she asked.

"You are so beautiful and I didn't think you would say yes," I replied. As we continued chatting we decided to go for dinner instead of just coffee.

We decided to go into the city for our first date. The tickets were already in my hand as I waited for her at the train station. It had been a long time since I had been on a date and this was the first time I'd done so since I'd been sober. I wanted to make sure I did things right, which normally was something that I never thought about when it came to dating.

We spent most of the day walking around the city, talking and sharing about our lives. I wanted her to know about my past.

During dinner, something came over me and I said out loud to her, "You know what I think? I think that you are going to be my wife and we are going to get married in April!" She laughed and asked how I could *possibly* know that. After I said it, I realized that I probably should *not* have said it.

As we continued dating, I could see she was nervous talking with me about marriage, especially since we barely knew each other. I assured her that I would take the time to get to know her. She agreed and then put me to the test. For the next three months, I was not to tell anyone we were dating. During that time, I had to show her what kind of person I really was. After that three-month period if we were still interested, then we could let others know. I told her we could take a whole year if she wanted, but I knew for sure, after that, she would be my wife.

Later on, I learned that Emily had been waiting on God to bring her the man that He had chosen for her. She had been praying for years. She also received a prophetic word that God would bring this man at an appointed time.

Months after we committed ourselves to each other, she shared with me that, right before I came into her life, she went on a missions trip to Poland with the women in her church. During that trip, the Lord began to show her that her appointed time had come. She knew, all the while she was flying home, that she would be soon meeting the man God had chosen for her. There was no coincidence that my first Sunday at Harvest Time Church was the Sunday that she was in Poland being prepared for what was to come. We were married April 27, 2012; exactly twenty-five years from the time she received that prophetic word as a girl graduating from high school.

I had never thought that I would get married again. I was married before, but during those years I was a drunk and really didn't have a marriage. Most of the time I was kicked out of the house and the marriage was short lived. The idea of getting married again never entered my mind. At one time I thought, "If I ever get married again, it will have to be to a strong woman of God." The Lord answered that prayer. He gave me a wife that would love me unconditionally and a wife that would be a support to me and be a family to me that I never really experienced.

The day I married Emily Houck was a day that Jehovah Nissi was waving a victory banner over me. He was declaring VICTORY, and restoring my life by giving me a family of my own. I had been sober over three years and the Lord had done so much for me.

> **Psalms 20:5**
> **"We will shout for joy when you are victorious and will lift up our banners in the name of our God. May the Lord grant all your request."(NIV)**

JEHOVAH NISSI MENU

Soup:
Minestrone Soup

Salad:
Classic Cucumber Salad

Fish Entree:
Grilled Fish Steaks

Meat Entree:
Herb Roasted Chicken

Vegetarian Dish:
Baba Ganoush

Dessert:
Nutty Brownies

Prayer:

*Thank you Father, Jehovah Nissi, who is my banner and victory.
I thank you for bringing me to this banqueting table and that you
placed a banner of love over my guest and me. Celebrate with us as
we eat this delicious food and dwell on the victories
that you brought us through.
Amen*

Minestrone Soup
(Serves 8)

½ cup organic Coconut Oil
1 cup of organic Spanish onions cut into small diced
1 cup of organic Celery cut into small diced
1 cup of organic Carrots cut into small diced
4 cups of organic Vegetables broth
2 (14 ounce) cans of organic whole peeled Tomatoes in juice
6 large organic Potatoes, peeled and cut into medium diced
6 cloves of organic Elephant Garlic chopped
2 cups of cook organic Tri-colors Pasta
6 teaspoons of organic Tomato Puree'
1 Tablespoon of organic All Purpose Seasoning
1 Tablespoon of organic dried Italian Herbs
1 teaspoon of organic kosher Sea Salt
1 teaspoon of organic Black Pepper
½ a bunch of organic Curly Parsley

1. In a 5-quart saucepan heat the oil and add the carrots, celery, and onions. Cook until they are soft, add the chopped garlic and brown it for about 5 minutes.
2. Add the tomatoes and the juice and the vegetable broth and bring it to a boil, add the potatoes and tomato puree' and cook the potatoes until they are soft lower the heat.
3. Add the rest of the ingredients keep cooking for 20 minutes and serve.

Classic Cucumber Salad
(Serves 8)

4 pound of organic European Cucumber cut into half moon
1 teaspoon of organic kosher Sea Salt
1 teaspoon of organic Black Pepper
1 Tablespoon of organic fresh Dill chopped

1 Tablespoon of organic fresh Cilantro chopped
½ cup of organic Sour Cream
½ cup of organic plain Yogurt
1 Tablespoon of organic Apple Cider Vinegar
1 Tablespoon of organic fresh Lemon Juice

1. In a large mixing bowl combine all the ingredients mix well let it sit for about 1 hour in the refrigerator and serve.

Grilled Fish Steaks
(Serves 8)

8 (7 oz.) fresh water Swordfish Steaks
1 teaspoons of organic kosher Sea Salt
1 teaspoons of organic Black Pepper
1 Tablespoons of organic Spanish Paprika
1 Tablespoon of organic Garlic Powder
1 Tablespoon of organic Onion Powder
1 Tablespoon of organic Mexican Ground Cumin
2 Tablespoons of organic fresh Italian Parley chopped
2 Tablespoons of organic fresh Cilantro chopped
½ of cup of organic fresh Lemon Juice
½ of cup of organic extra- virgin Olive Oil

1. In a large mixing bowl place the fish and add all the ingredients make sure you coated each piece well.
2. Grill Swordfish steaks at medium heat and cook for 5 minutes each side or until they are firmly done serve.

Herb Roasted Chicken

Herb Roasted Chicken
(Serves 8)

4 whole roasting Chickens about 4 pound each, cut into 8 pieces
3 Tablespoons of organic Garlic Powder
1 teaspoons of organic kosher Sea Salt
1 teaspoons of organic Black Pepper
3 Tablespoons of organic Spanish Paprika
2 Tablespoons of organic fresh Rosemary chopped
1 Tablespoons of organic fresh Oregano chopped
1 Tablespoons of organic fresh Thyme
2 Tablespoons of organic fresh Parley chopped
½ cup of organic extra- virgin Olive Oil

1. Rinse the chicken parts, put into a large bowl and add all ingredients mix well rub the chicken well.
2. Place the well rub chicken into a large roasting pan into the oven at 350°F for 45 minutes or until done and serve hot.

Baba Ganoush
(Serves 8)
4 medium Japanese Eggplant cut into medium dice, and peeled
1 cup of organic fresh Lemon Juice
1 cup of organic Tahini
4 Tablespoons of chopped organic Elephant Garlic
3 Tablespoons of organic Olive Oil
1 teaspoon of organic kosher Sea Salt
1 teaspoon of organic Black Pepper
1 cup of organic Italian Fresh Parley chopped
1 large Bag of organic Pita Chips (optional)

1. Roast the eggplant in the oven at 350° F for 30 minutes or until golden brown and soft.
2. In a 7 Cup food processor put the eggplant and all the ingredients except the parley. Puree the mix until smooth then chopped the parley and add it in and serve.

Nutty Brownies
(Serves 8)

7 Squares of organic unsweetened Chocolate
1 stick of organic Butter
3 cups of organic Sugar
6 organic brown Eggs
2 cups of organic Almond Flour
1 Tablespoon of organic Vanilla extract
2 cups of organic Almonds chopped
1 cup of organic white Chocolate Chips
1 cup of organic dark Chocolate Chips

1. Melt both chocolate dark and white and butter together over low heat in a small saucepan.
2. Beat together sugar and eggs blend in the chocolate mixture, stir in the flour and the remaining ingredients and mixed well.
3. Pour into a 6" baking pan baked at 350°F for 45 minutes cool then down and cut into small squares.

JEHOVAH SHALOM
The Lord My Peace

Chapter Eleven

JEHOVAH SHALOM
The Lord My Peace

Jeremiah 29:11 "I know the plans that I have for you declares Yahweh. They are plans for peace and not disaster, plans to give you a future filled with hope."

I was growing so much in my faith, and God was restoring more and more back to me. By now I was working as a chef in a corporate setting. This was something I thought would never happen.

One day, I ran into one of my Jewish friends, Noah, who was looking for a chef to work at a Jewish academy. I had worked for him before, but I was a heavy drinker at the time. Now he needed a chef to oversee the cafeteria at the school. Understandably, he was concerned about my drinking habits. "I don't drink any more," I told him. "I'm a Christian!"

"That's great!" he replied.

A Jewish rabbi was happy that I was a Christian? Wow!

We spoke about another friend, Nieves, who had worked for him. Nieves still worked for him, Noah said, but he was still drinking a lot. Nieves and I used to party together quite heavily. We would drink and party until the wee hours of the morning, then go to work together.

When I told Nieves, after arriving at the academy, that I wasn't drinking any more, he couldn't believe it. I would find him staring at me from a distance. I constantly looked for ways to reach out to him but it wasn't easy. He was still drinking quite heavily.

About three weeks into working at the academy, Nieves stopped me and asked, "How did you do it? How did you stop drinking? Tell me!"

"I can't tell you now," I said. "I need to get the French fries across the street. I'll tell you when I get back."

I went across the street to the Jewish market, which was owned by Noah. When I returned, there were a number of police cars and an ambulance in front of the school. I went in, and my friend, Nieves, was unconscious on the floor, bleeding from his nose and ears. My heart sank!

I tried to go and pray for him while the medical team was working on him but I couldn't reach him. Later that evening, I received a text that he had passed away.

The next morning, Noah and I began to talk about Nieves. Noah said to me, "You were trying to reach him. I could tell by your eyes that you were trying to reach him." But unfortunately I didn't!

I don't know why I didn't stop to take the time to tell Nieves about Jesus, my Shalom. Things might have turned out differently if I had. I struggled for the next several weeks with guilt because I hadn't stopped to tell him about my faith in Jesus Christ. Satan would throw arrows of condemnation at me. It was horrible.

Thankfully, in spite of all the enemy was doing to attack me with guilt, Jehovah Shalom was there, showering me with peace and comfort, a peace that passed all understanding, helping me make it through the torment. He reminded me that, apart from His mercy and grace, I could have been Nieves. I could have been the one sprawled out on the floor, blood flowing from my face.

I don't know why salvation was granted to me and not Nieves, but I knew one thing for sure: I would never miss another opportunity to share the Gospel or to tell an alcoholic how I was set free from addiction. No matter where I was or whom I was with, I made a decision that I would not be ashamed of the Gospel.

When you accept Jesus Christ as your Lord and King, the Holy Spirit, who is the third person of the Trinity, comes and resides in you. The Holy Spirit is the one who gives you that Shalom peace, that sense of well-being which keeps your heart steady even when everything in the natural should make you quake in your boots. That's why the Scriptures call it "the peace that passes all understanding." You shouldn't be at peace, but you are!

There is something else that can occur to believers, which also will give you great strength and wisdom. It's called the infilling or baptism of the Holy Spirit.

One Wednesday night, Pastor Nick, the associate pastor at Harvest Time, gave a teaching on the Baptism of the Holy Spirit. At the end of the service, he invited those who wanted to receive it to come to the altar. I'd never experienced that before, and I wanted more of God, so I went forward. As people began praying for me, I felt something like an electric surge go through my body. Shortly thereafter, I began to speak in an unknown tongue. My mouth was speaking faster than I could think, and something I can only describe as shalom peace came over me! It was so wonderful! I had never experienced anything like it!

After receiving the baptism of the Holy Spirit, I noticed that my faith was elevated to a different level. Revelations from God came more readily and clearly. It was like a 3D light bulb was switched on high. Everything became alive in greater measure. My faith walk was so much deeper. My understanding was increased. It was amazing!

Many Christians are afraid of the baptism of the Holy Spirit but, personally, I don't see how your faith can grow without it.

One of the revelations that came to me after being baptized with the Holy Spirit was a command to write this book. It was a Wednesday and I was feeling this nudge that I needed to go to church that evening. I was feeling it all day long. When I came home from work, I told my wife about it. She was not feeling very well that night, but I insisted that we go, so we did.

Soon after we arrived, I felt the need to go somewhere by myself and pray. I started pacing back and forth in the row where we were sitting. Then I said to the Lord, "You got me here. What do you need to tell me?"

A few minutes later, I heard the word, "twelve", then the word "names." Then the Lord indicated He was referring to the twelve names of God in Hebrew. Then I heard the word, "cookbook."

"What does a cookbook have to do with the twelve names of God?" I wondered.

During the service that night, I got what I'd call a "download from heaven," telling me just what the book was supposed to say and how to organize it. I was floored! I'd never experienced any communication from God like this before.

Weeks and months passed, but the vision never left me. It remained fresh and alive in my heart. Despite the "download from heaven," I truly wondered how this book would ever get written. I didn't know how to write a book. I didn't even know where to start. There were moments when I thought the project was too big for me, even an impossibility. Yet I could not get the vision out of my mind.

Then one day, Tommy Barnett, founder of the Dream Center, a ministry to the homeless and other isolated people in Los Angeles, CA (www.dreamcenter.org), came to speak at our church's men's conference.

His first sermon was entitled, "When Your Dream Is Bigger than You." "Wow," I thought, "that's definitely how I feel about writing this book. This is so much bigger than me."

I listened intently as Tommy spoke, knowing the topic he was speaking about wasn't delivered by accident, but by the hand of God. "If your dream is bigger than you," Tommy said, "then it is from God. If this dream keeps poking you, then you know it is from God."

I ran up to him after the service ended. I told him the Lord had asked me to write a book. It didn't make sense to me, I said, but I couldn't get it out of my mind.

"Tell me about this book," he said. Once I did, he replied, "Son you *have* to write this book." After I left that conference, I felt so empowered and full of faith. I knew that this book was going to be written.

That's when I began to tell others about my plans. "I'm going to write a cookbook based on the 12 names of God," I said. My wife supported me, even though she didn't fully understand the concept. She simply said "Okay." Some friends just gave me blank stares. Some laughed and said, "Oh, Julio…."

I'd hoped for a more enthusiastic response. I freely admit that. Even without it, however, the vision God gave me was still throbbing with life, the nudge of the Holy Spirit persistent and insistent. I knew this book was going to be written because God, the author and finisher of my faith, had said so.

Without question, I could not have written this book without the peace and assurance from my Jehovah Shalom. Having the Holy Spirit in my life had birthed greater things in me and through me than I had ever imagined He would.

He can do the same for you, if you will allow Him to do so. He will give you dreams and visions that far surpass your comprehension. Just believe, step out in faith, and He will give you the grace and empowerment to do the impossible in your life.

John 14:27 "Peace I leave with you, My peace I give to you; not as the world give do I give you. Let not your heart be troubled, neither let it be afraid."

JEHOVAH SHALOM MENU

Soup:
Chilled Coconut Cucumber Soup

Salad:
Avocado & Red Onion
Pineapple Salad

Fish Entree:
Sea Bass Rosa Style

Meat Entree:
Beef Stew

Vegetarian Dish:
Ratatouille

Dessert:
Coconut Pudding

Prayer:

We come to you Jehovah Shalom, our God who is our Peace. We invite you to be our Peace today as we gather together in your name and ask you to bless our food and our fellowship.
Amen

Chilled Coconut Cucumber Soup
(Serves 8)

4 medium organic peeled Cucumber
3 small organic Shallots cut into small diced
1 half of organic fresh Fennel cut into small diced
3 cups of organic vegan coconut water
1 teaspoon of organic fresh Dill finely chopped
3 cups of organic Coconut Milk
1 teaspoon of organic Mexican Cilantro finely chopped
2 Tablespoons of organic raw Honey
½ teaspoon organic low salt Soy Sauce
1 teaspoon of organic kosher Sea Salt
1 teaspoon of organic White Pepper

1. Place the cucumbers, shallots, fennel, coconut water and dill and cilantro in a blender puree' until smooth. Add the coconut milk and the rest of the ingredients combined and whisk together cover and chilled for one hour.

Avocado and Red Onion Pineapple Salad
(Serves 8)

1 cup of organic Vegetable Oil
1 cup of organic Apple Cider Vinegar
1 cup of organic fresh mango Orange Juice
½ cup of organic Sugar
1 teaspoon of organic kosher Sea Salt
1 teaspoon of organic Black Pepper
8 cups of organic fresh Boston lettuce, hand torn
2 cups of organic Pineapple small diced
2 cups of organic sweet Red onion, slice thinly
4 Tablespoons organic fresh Lime Juice
3 organic Mexican Avocados, small diced

1. In a blender combine all ingredients, except lettuce, pine-apple, onions and avocados. Blend until smooth.
2. In a large bowl toss together the lettuce, pineapple, red onions and avocados and add the oil dressing to it and serve into 8 salad plates.

Sea Bass Rosa Style
(Serves 8)

8 (8oz.) fresh water organic sea Bass Fillets
4 organic Tomatoes small diced
4 Tablespoon of organic raw Coconut Oil
1 teaspoon of organic kosher Sea Salt
1 teaspoon of organic Black Pepper
5 Tablespoon of organic Shallots minced
1 cup of organic kosher non-alcoholic White Wine
4 Tablespoon of organic Fish stock
1 cup of organic Heavy Cream
4 Tablespoon of organic fresh Scallions chopped
1 organic Lemon cut into 8 wedges

1. In a large roasting pan at medium heat, add the oil heat for about 2 minutes.
2. Add the fish fillets and sear them for about 2 minutes each side, add the shallots cook for about 3 minutes until golden brown, remove the fish put it aside.
3. Deglaze the pan with the non-alcoholic white wine then add the fish stock reduce for about 2 minutes then add the heavy cream and tomatoes and salt and pepper and add the fish to the sauce.
4. Cook all together until the fish is firm and the sauce is reduced by half, serve each fillet and topped it with Rosa sauce and chopped scallions and lemon wedges.

Beef Stew
(Serves 8)

3 pounds of organic grass feed Tenderloin Tips trimmed and cut in 1- inch cubes
1 Tablespoon of organic Spanish Paprika
2 organic Green Peppers, medium cut
2 cups of organic canned dice Tomatoes in juice
2 organic Spanish Onions medium cut
2 Tablespoons of organic virgin Olive Oil
6 organic medium potatoes peeled and cube in 1-inch chunks
2 organic Bay Leaves
2 Tablespoons of organic minced Garlic
½ bunch of organic flat Italian Parsley finely chopped
2 cups of organic beef broth

1. Brown beef tips in oil.
2. When partly cooked add green pepper, onions bay leaves and garlic and paprika.
3. Cook with tomatoes over medium heat for 20 minutes place potatoes with meat and tomatoes in large saucepan and add the beef broth. Cook for about 30 minutes, garnish with the parsley and serve.

Ratatouille
(Serves 8)

2 cups of organic extra-virgin Olive Oil
2 cups of organic Spanish Onions medium diced
1 cup of organic green Bell Peppers medium diced
1 cup of organic Red Bell Peppers medium diced
1 cup of organic Yellow Squash
1 cup of organic Zucchini
2 cups of organic Japanese Eggplant
4 cups of organic Plum Tomatoes chopped
2 Tablespoons of organic Mince Garlic

1 teaspoon organic kosher Sea Salt
1 teaspoon of organic Black Pepper
2 Tablespoons of organic fresh Thyme chopped
2 Tablespoons of organic fresh Oregano chopped
2 Tablespoons of organic fresh Basil chopped
3 organic Bay leaves

1. Mixed all ingredients spread them evenly on to a roasting sheet pans.
2. Pre heat the oven at 350°F put sheet pan with vegetable a roast them for about 30 minutes or until they are done golden brown.
3. Remove the bay leaves and serve at room temperature or chilled.

Coconut Pudding
(Serves 8)

2 cups of organic Sugar
3 cups of organic Coconut Water
3 cups of the Almond Milk
1 cups of organic Coconut Shavings
6 organic brown Eggs lightly beating
1 Tablespoon of organic Cinnamon
2 Tablespoons of Rum Flavoring

1. Cook the coconut water and sugar to a syrup stage. When sugar syrup reaches this stage, using a candy thermometer the syrup temperature should reach between 230°F and 235°F.
2. Add the coconut shaving, milk, cinnamon and rum flavoring. Then stir in the egg yolks. Cook stirring constantly until the mixture is thick.
3. Pour into serving soufflé cups torch the top until golden brown and serve chilled.

ADONAY
The Lord My Master

Chapter Twelve

ADONAY
The Lord, My Master

Psalms 62:11-12 "Elohim has spoken once, I have heard it said twice: 'Power belongs to Elohim. Mercy belongs to you, O Adonay."

During the time I was homeless, I lost all forms of identification – my driver's license, my green card, and my social security card. Someone picked my pocket and took my wallet while I was sleeping on the bench.

Once in rehab, I was given a New York State Benefit Card. That was the only card of identification that I had for a few years.

Soon after I met Emily, she helped me start the process of getting the rest of my identification restored. The process wasn't easy. At times it felt like the enemy wanted to erase my identity completely, as though it never existed. At times I would get discouraged and feel like giving up because the situation looked so impossible. Even so, we would continue to pray and believe that God would restore what the enemy had taken away.

Finally, I hired an immigration lawyer to help with the process. Even with his help, it took months and months to resolve everything. Even then, I had to wait. In fact, it wasn't until I was married that all forms of identification were replaced.

God had a purpose for this time of waiting, however. (He always does.) During this time, My Lord and Master refined me, giving me a new identity. The old Julio was stomped out and the new Julio, a new creature in Christ, emerged. Here was one thing the enemy could never take away – not just a "me" restored by the power of my Heavenly Father, but a "me" with an even greater identity, the one I hold in Him.

While I was working for the Hilton Hotel chain, other chefs would talk about getting their Certified Executive Chef (CEC) certification with the American Culinary Federation (ACF). I used to think about becoming certified but never thought it was within my reach.

One summer I moved to central New York where I found work with a state university. Upon hire, I was asked if I would be interested in obtaining my CEC. Without a thought, I replied with a resounding "Yes."

I was so excited. I couldn't wait to get home so I could tell my wife. When I did, she replied, "God is restoring forgotten dreams in your life."

She was right. I had dreamed of getting my certification for a very long time; now that dream was about to become reality.

Preparing for my certification exam was intense. I practiced and practiced every facet of preparing and cooking the three-course meal I had selected to show the judges who would evaluate my skills. I had to incorporate four different kinds of cuts, as well as prepare a couple of different classical sauces. Each part of my meal would also be judged on taste and serving size. The sizes had to be exact!

As the day for my exam approached, I was feeling nervous. I faced much adversity, as the enemy allowed whatever negative thing he could find to be stirred up against me in the days and weeks leading up to my big day. I even began to doubt that I would pass. Many chefs had told me that a lot of people do not pass on the first try.

My wife and I prayed and fasted several days leading up to the day of the exam. The night before the exam, I couldn't sleep. I needed to pass, as this was my only chance to see a dream fulfilled. Many of my co-workers were saying to me, "Julio, you have to pass this!"

Finally, I decided: "Whether I pass this test or not, I will praise my Master Chef, Jesus Christ." I continued to have confidence in God, however, and believed I would, indeed, pass it. I would get my certification.

On the day of the exam, I got up early and prayed with my wife. I also checked every list of ingredients and equipment twice. I wanted to make sure that I had everything I needed with me.

There were four other candidates who were taking their exam that day. I was scheduled to take the exam last. As I waited for the others to finish, I felt like a woman getting ready to give birth. In fact, I *was* giving birth — to a dream, a dream that I thought would never come to pass. As my time to take the exam drew near, I started getting really nervous again. Then it was show time.

The pressure was on, and next three hours were devoted to doing the best cooking I had ever done in my life. I would make the following dishes:

Fish Dish–Grilled Salmon topped with steamed Maine Lobster Scampi served on a bed of garlic parsnip puree.

Salad Dish–Hand-torn Boston lettuce with globe artichoke hearts, oven roasted grape tomatoes and braised Belgian Endives, topped with smoke bacon and sautéed julienne Bartlett pears tossed with Brunoise pear Dijon mustard Vinaigrette.

Main Course – Pan Roasted Chicken Supreme topped with natural fines herbs au jus and served with small-diced roasted Rosemary Potatoes, sautéed garlic baby spinach and red peppers and glazed dill rondelle carrots.

Every facet of preparation and cooking was timed. I had a timekeeper telling me where I was with the time, when I needed to plate the food and so forth. Taking this exam reminded me of one of the shows where you have so many minutes to prepare your meal and everyone is wondering if you are going to make it.

At one point, during the last hour of the exam, I felt my body getting tired. Then, all of a sudden, I felt this surge of energy go through my body. (Unbeknownst to me, my wife and her friends were praying for me right then, asking God to supply me with supernatural strength.)

At the very end, I pushed through, working faster and faster to make sure every meal was done. Then I heard," Time, chef!" and I was done. Praise the Lord I was done. I fell on my knees, as I was so exhausted mentally, physically and emotionally.

A few moments later, the three judges came in. "Let's go into the board room to review your dishes," they said. They started off by saying that they had a couple of concerns. My heart sank. "This does not look good," I thought.

One of the grilled salmon was an ounce too many, they said. Secondly, the same size plate was also used for every dish, something they didn't like, so they were taking two points off for these reasons.

Was my certification in jeopardy, I wondered? Did I fail? I was concerned.

The lead judge then said to one of the others: "Would you tell him already? He looks like he's going to cry!" The other judge held out his hand, shook mine, and said, "Congratulations! You passed your CEC exam! Welcome to the ACF!"

I took off my chef hat and started crying. As I was crying, I said, "You don't know the road that I travelled to get here!" All the judges around the table started tearing up.

In their final evaluation, the judges said they loved the different flavors that were put together, as well as the whole presentation of my dishes. On my passing grade form, they wrote that my presentation was the best of the day. Adonay, My Lord, my Master, had restored my dream, one that I thought was long gone, just as He promised!

When I came out of the boardroom, Christina, a photographer who had been taking pictures of my food from the beginning, that first chef table, right up to the last and during the exam, was there waiting for me. "Well, did you pass?" she asked.

I didn't have to say anything. I just raised both my hands in victory. Before I really knew what was going on, Christina started bawling. That's when I realized she had been as much a part of this journey as I had been. She shared my struggles and now she shared my victory.

As I was packing my things, the lead judge came to me and pointed to the sleeve of my chef coat." I like your fish," he said. He then told me that he was a pastor of a church. Before the day of my exam, I had put on the arm of my chef jacket the Christian fish sign. To have that sign on my jacket meant that I was not the same chef I had been years ago; I was now a chef representing my Lord. It then occurred to me that the Lord sent one of His servants to be the top judge for my exam.

When Christ is your Master, King of your life, He goes before you and prepares the way for you. No matter what comes against you, Christ, your Lord will lead the way. It is only Him that can bring true success and honor. When you honor Him, He will honor you!

Nothing illustrates this more for me than the day I took my wife to visit the rehabilitation facility where I lived for so many months.

Most of the staff still worked there and recognized me right away. They could not believe how well I looked. The residence nurse commented that I must be still on medications to be doing so well and looking this good. I told her that I wasn't on any medication. I simply had become a believer in Jesus Christ. She was shocked and asked me if I had any cravings. I told her no. She said, "Wow, that is amazing, and to think that you were on some heavy medications." The staff could not get over the transformation that had occurred in my life.

I then inquired about other residents who had been there the same time that I was. After reciting each name, the staff told me that they were either back in the program, had committed suicide, or were in jail. Not one person I mentioned was doing well. I was the only one who had made it.

On the way home, Emily and I talked about our visit, and especially how well things had turned out for me, as compared with everyone else. "Why me?" I wondered. "Why was my outcome so different?" The answer, we decided, was Jesus Christ. He allowed me to experience total freedom from something that had me so bound. He made all the difference!

As I reflect back on my journey – where I began on the streets of New York to where I am now, a certified executive chef — I realize that I would not be where I am today if not for having Adonay, my Lord and Master, on the throne of my life. Truly He has become Elohim, My Creator; Jehovah Rapha, My Healer; El Roi, the One who watches over me; Jehovah Shammah, the One who is there/His abiding presence; Ruach Qodesh, my Holy Spirit; Jehovah Tsidkenu, My Righteousness: Jehovah Jireh, My Provider; Go-el, My Redeemer; Jehovah Tsur, My Rock; Jehovah Shalom, My Peace; and Adonay, My Lord and Master.

With this new identity, He gave me a great wife who loves me unconditionally and supports me. Truly she is my helpmate. He provided for me in ways you cannot even imagine. He restored my dreams and passions. He led me down paths I couldn't even dream about. He redeemed my life and transformed it to be something far greater than it had been before. He gave me peace beyond my own comprehension.

If you have not received Christ as your Lord and Savior, You can do it today. God's redeeming power is available to you right now, just as it was there for me, the day I cried "I need You, Jesus.". Romans 10:9 says, "If you declare that Yeshua is Lord and believe that God brought him back to life, you will be saved." By believing, you receive God's approval, and by declaring your faith in Him, you are saved. Scripture says, "Whoever believes in Him will not be ashamed." (Romans 10: 11)

The beginning step is to ask Jesus Christ into your life and ask Him to become your Lord and Master. He desires to be Lord of your life and wants to glorify His name through you. If you want this same Jesus to come and live inside you, to be your Lord and Savior as He is mine, then say this prayer out loud:

Dear Lord, I confess that I am a sinner. I have done many things that don't please you. I come to you now to repent and ask you to forgive my sins. I believe that you died on the cross for me, to save me. I ask you now to come into my life and be Lord and Master of my life. Help me to live every day in a way that pleases you. I love you, Lord, and I thank you that you came so that I can live my life abundantly and to the full. Amen

Psalms 86:15 "But you O Adonay, are a compassionate and merciful God. You are patient, always faithful and ready to forgive."

ADONAY MENU

Soup:
Cream of Broccoli

Salad:
Hearty Asian Veggie Salad

Fish Entree:
*Pan-Seared Rainbow Trout
topped with Brown Butter*

Meat Entree:
Chicken Fricassee

Vegetarian Dish:
Baked Zucchini Casserole

Dessert:
Chocolate Pudding

Prayer:

*We call upon you Adonay, who is our Lord. We declare that
you are King and Master over our lives. This is the day that you
have made and we will rejoice and be glad. We gather together to
celebrate your goodness and love that you have given us.*
Amen

Cream of Broccoli
(Serves 8)

2 pounds of organic fresh Broccoli
6 ounces of organic White Sharp Cheddar Cheese
3 cups of organic Vegetable Broth
3 cups of organic Almond Soymilk
½ cup of organic curly Parsley chopped
½ cup of organic Green Onions finely chopped
1 Tablespoon of organic Garlic powder
1 Tablespoon organic Onion Powder
1 teaspoon of organic kosher Sea Salt
1 teaspoon of organic White Pepper

1. In 5-quart saucepan heat the vegetable broth, soymilk and broccoli bring it to a boil until the broccoli is tender. Simmer on low heat for about 15 minutes.
2. With a hand blender or food processor puree broccoli in the saucepan together with all the liquid at slow speed, blend in the rest of the ingredients. Cook the soup for about 15 minutes and serve.

Hearty Asian Veggie Salad
(Serves 8)

2 pounds of fresh organic Stir-fry Vegetables
2 Tablespoons of organic Sesame Oil
4 Tablespoons organic Teriyaki Sauce
2 Tablespoons of organic Soy Sauce
16 Cups of organic fresh Spinach Leaves
8 teaspoons of organic Balsamic Vinegar

1. In a large skillet heat sesame oil and soy sauce over medium-high heat.
2. Bring it to a simmer then add the vegetables sautéed until they are crisp-tender about 6 minutes.

160

3. Take the vegetables and toss with the raw spinach and portion in to 8 cold salad bowls, and drizzle the balsamic vinegar on each salad and serve.

Pan-seared Rainbow Trout topped with Brown Butter Sauce
(Serves 8)

8 (8oz.) organic trout Fillets
6 Tablespoons of organic brown all-purpose Flour
1 Tablespoons of organic fresh Lemon Juice
12 oz of organic whole Butter
1 Tablespoon of organic Coconut Raw Oil
1 teaspoon of organic kosher Sea Salt
1 teaspoon of organic Black Pepper
5 Tablespoon of fresh organic Italian Chopped Parley
½ cup of organic kosher Non-Alcoholic White Wine

1. Take the trout fillets and season each piece with Salt and pepper. Roll in flour.
2. Heat the butter and oil in large skillet over medium heat. In batches, sauté the trout until golden brown and cooked through, 4 to 5 minutes each side. Remove the fish from the skillet and keep warm while making the sauce.
3. De-glazed the skillet with the non-alcoholic wine, add the butter and cook butter over medium heat until lightly brown with a nutty aroma 4 to 5 minutes.
4. Add lemon juice and reduce for about 2 minutes. Pour the sauce over the fish fillets, add a little parsley to each fish and serve.

Chicken Fricassee
(Serves 8)

4 organic whole Chicken cut into 8 pieces each
4 Tablespoons of organic Lemon Juice
10 organic garlic Cloves minced
2 organic Spanish Onions chopped into medium dice
4 organic Idaho Potatoes, peeled and cut into medium chunks
2 (8-ounce) cans of organic Tomato sauce
1 Tablespoon of organic ground Cumin
4 organic Bay Leaves
1 cups of organic Coconut Oil
1 cup of organic sliced green Olives
1 cup of organic golden Raisins
1 cup of organic Capers
1 cup of organic kosher Non-Alcoholic Red Wine
1 teaspoon of organic kosher Sea Salt
1 teaspoon of organic Black Pepper

1. Marinate the chicken in lemon juice and seasoning for 2 hours. Heat the coconut oil in a large skillet and add the chicken cook until golden brown.
2. Add the onions, garlic, bay leaves, cumin and tomato sauce.
3. When onions are almost tender, add potatoes, raisins, and capers.
4. Cook over low heat until chicken is tender, stir in the non-alcoholic red wine and cook for about 25 minutes over medium heat, or until the chicken reaches 165°F the serve.

Baked Zucchini Casserole

Baked Zucchini Casserole
(Serves 8)

3 Tablespoons of organic unsalted Butter
½ of organic Spanish Onion cut into small dice
2 Tablespoons of organic Garlic finely minced
4 pounds of organic Zucchini cut into large chunks
1 teaspoon of organic kosher Sea Salt
1 teaspoon of organic Black Pepper
3 cups of organic shredded sharp Cheddar Cheese
2 cups of organic Japanese Panko Breadcrumbs
3 cups of organic Tomato Sauce

1. In a large skillet or frying pan, heat the butter and oil.
2. Sautéed the onion garlic and zucchini cook until tender, add the salt and pepper.
3. Layer the mixture and add the tomato sauce and cheese on each layer into a 2-quart casserole pan.

4. Topped the casserole with the Japanese Panko breadcrumb. Baked at 350°F for 30 minutes. Let it sit for about 15 minutes at room temperature and serve.

Chocolate Pudding
(Serves 8)

2 cups of organic all-purpose Flour
2 cups of organic Sugar
7 Tablespoons of organic Cocoa Powder
3 Tablespoons of organic Coconut Raw Oil
3 teaspoons of organic Baking Powder
1 cup of organic soy Almond Milk
1 teaspoons of organic Vanilla Bean Extract
1 cup of organic chopped Walnuts
1 cup of organic Brown Sugar
2 cups of Water

1. Mix all ingredients together in a 4-quart casserole, topped with the chopped walnuts.
2. Baked for about 1 hour at 325°F.
3. Cool before serving.

Chef Julio Rubio

*C*hef Julio Rubio has been in the culinary business for over 23 years. He started working with the Hilton International UK under the apprenticeship of several European chefs and obtained expertise in various global cuisines, holding several titles over the years, including Executive Chef and Corporate Chef, and cooking for countless individuals and groups in the secular arena.

Out of the depths of despair, sleeping on the streets of NYC, Chef Julio overcame his addiction to alcohol through his personal journey of faith and hope through Jesus Christ. Now being restored, he is using his culinary expertise for the Lord, his personal Master Chef.

Chef Julio currently resides in Connecticut with his lovely wife Emily and their dog, Sashie.

Chef Julio Rubio is available for speaking engagements, cooking demonstrations and events. Contact www.master-chefministries.com for more information.